HEALING

THE

HEART

OF

CONFLICT

ALSO BY MARC GOPIN

Between Eden and Armageddon
Holy War, Holy Peace

HEALING
THE
HEART
OF
CONFLICT

8 CRUCIAL STEPS

TO MAKING PEACE

WITH YOURSELF

AND OTHERS

MARC GOPIN

RODALE

Notice

Mention of specific companies, organizations, or authorities in this book does not imply endorsement by the publisher, nor does mention of specific companies, organizations, or authorities in the book imply that they endorse the book.

Internet addresses and telephone numbers given in this book were accurate at the time the book went to press.

Please note that names and even genders have been changed in the stories in order to protect the reputations and good work of colleagues, students, congregants, and advisees.

Printed in the United States of America
Rodale Inc. makes every effort to use acid-free ∞, recycled paper ♻.

Book design by DesignWorks

Library of Congress Cataloging-in-Publication Data

Gopin, Marc.
    Healing the heart of conflict : 8 crucial steps to making peace with yourself and others / Marc Gopin.
        p.   cm.
    ISBN 1–57954–793–1 hardcover
    1. Conflict management.   2. Conflict (Psychology)   3. Spirituality.   I. Title.
HM1126.G66   2004
303.6'9—dc22   2004014620

Distributed to the trade by Holtzbrinck Publishers

2   4   6   8   10   9   7   5   3   1   hardcover

WE **INSPIRE** AND **ENABLE** PEOPLE TO IMPROVE
THEIR LIVES AND THE WORLD AROUND THEM

To Alexandra Rose,
my daughter Lexi:

Shoshanat Ya'acov,
Rose of Jacob,
Flower of my father's heart,
Petal of his departing soul,
You sprung into his youth,
Into his strength against all odds.
I held your tiny body on the emergency room gurney,
With your pneumonia-laden lungs,
Wires and tubes interlacing our bodies.
I held you in between my legs as we lay down,
And I gave birth to you,
As a little of me died,
As they rescued you.
And now you are strong as an ox,
Like Dad, fiercely strong,
With calm, haughty eyes,
A delicious belly laugh,
And astonishing beauty,
That lights up all of God's worlds.
Thank God for you,
Thank God for every moment of you.
Be a fearless healer,
My beloved Lexi.
Heal all of God's worlds,
No matter how benighted.
I will be with you forever,
When you seek me here,
My sweetest Rose.

ACKNOWLEDGMENTS

I would like to thank the publishers and editors at Rodale, particularly Stephanie Tade and Marc Jaffe, and especially Chris Potash, for believing in this project, showing so much respect to me, and combining the business of publishing with transformative work for the good of society. Esmond Harmsworth, my agent, has shepherded this project from its inception and has given positive forms of encouragement that spurred me to persist in the creation of this book. I recommend him as an agent, and I owe him more than I can say. I also am pleased to thank Rochelle Silver, a wonderful and creative agent, who so generously encouraged my work and shepherded me into formal work with Esmond and the publishers.

There are a variety of colleagues and fellow travelers who have taught me so much over the years, and who, in a variety of ways, helped me along the path toward creating this book. They include Scott Appleby, Kevin Avruch, Sara Cobb, Nancy Good Sider, Ron Kraybill, John Paul Lederach, Martha Minnow, Marc Ross, Richard E. Rubenstein, Lisa Schirch, Donald Shriver, David Smock, my fellow faculty members at the Institute for Conflict Analysis and Resolution, George Mason University, and the faculty of the Conflict Transformation Program at Eastern Mennonite University.

There are a few people who believed in my work and have supported me along the way. They also happen to be inspiring examples of thoughtful, creative contributors to the entire field of healing conflicts without whom my ideas on these issues would be far less developed, and they include Rabbi Rachel Cowan and Libby Hoffman.

There are precious friends who have inspired me, encouraged me, and fixed me when I was down, and they include Aviva Bock, Robert Eisen, Bryan Hamlin, Ted Kaptchuk, Yehezkel Landau, Jack Lewis, Merri Menuskin, Joe Montville, Yoel Tobin, my sister Reissa Leigh, and Ted Sasson.

The staffs of two organizations that I have worked with have given me two homes in which to learn so much and to share with them my ideas, and they include the staffs of Facing History and Ourselves, especially Margo Strom, Adam Strom, Marc Skvirsky, and Marty Sleeper, as well as the staff of Initiatives of Change, especially Dick and Rande Ruffin, Marianne and Christoph Spreng, Charles and Kathy Aquilina, and Anne Hamlin.

My student Judy Dunbar made amazingly precise contributions to editing the manuscript and was a pleasure to work with, and Heather Woodman, the administrator of our new Center for World Religions, Diplomacy and Conflict

Resolution, was masterful in running my life in such a way that I could finish this book. Her friendship and spiritual guidance inspire me and many others.

My mother, Pauline Gopin, put up with my many absences from home duties such as washing the dishes, and she has my eternal gratitude for opening up her home to me and my family for five wonderful years of successful coexistence during which this book was written. We are only sorry that we had to move. Without that home base I am not sure I would have had the presence of mind to write.

As usual the greatest burden has been carried by my wonderful wife of eighteen years, Robyn, and my children, Ruthie, Lexi, and Isaac, as they have to deal with a man who has two jobs: 1) difficult peace work, and 2) the strange life of a writer, neither of which have been terribly convenient with three little children. Thank you, Robyn, from the bottom of my heart, for believing in me and the work, and for the exhaustion of making space for this in our lives. Someday we will not be tired anymore, and we will enjoy the fruit of these years.

CONTENTS

PART TWO: THE EIGHT STEPS APPLIED

INTRODUCTION

L
ong ago, even as a child, I was the one who made peace in my family. As I grew older this intuition for healing hurtful conflict merged in my mind with the ethical and spiritual goal of reducing suffering in the world. Since then I have spent my professional career teaching, negotiating, and traveling to the Middle East, Asia, Northern Ireland, and other global trouble spots to become involved in some of the world's most difficult geopolitical situations. I have engaged activists, politicians, military officers, diplomats, and extremists. I have trained thousands of students in the United States and overseas, and I continue these trainings to this day. At the same time, I have served the Jewish community several times as a rabbi, helping my congregants work through the everyday business and family conflicts that disrupt so many of our lives. The perspective gained from all these roles has lead to some conclusive insights into conflict in its many forms.

What I have discovered is that there is a fundamental similarity between the intractable feuds among rival nations that cause so much strife in the world and the destructive personal and family struggles that affect us so deeply as individuals. While the scale and the stakes are obviously very different, the underlying process, the drama, is the same.

The type of conflict I'm most concerned about is the complicated, ingrained style of fighting that drains us of our energy and serves no useful purpose (although the Eight Steps can be used to promote healing under any circumstances). This is in part because our minor arguments and disagreements are just that—minor. In fact, experience has taught me that minor disagreements are often quite healthy, and a diversity of opinions prod us to make creative decisions, to see the big picture, to achieve our potential—in a word, they can be constructive.

Unlike the ups and downs of everyday life, however, *destructive* conflicts are those that harm us on an ongoing basis and resist solution seemingly at every turn. Like the clash between a cold father and an angry son, or between sisters whose mutual love has turned to bitter jealousy, or between business partners and close friends whose amity has turned into distrust, or between neighbors from different races, ethnicities, or religions who have grown up filled with hate, destructive conflicts are based on primal emotions and cannot be solved by rational discussion and negotiation. Indeed, what goes on *between* people cannot be separated from what is going on *within* people. Who we are, deep inside, will determine how well we get along with others, and so, if we want to fix our conflicts, or anyone else's for that matter, we had better get started on ourselves.

The deepest causes of most conflicts, I've discovered, are feelings like dishonor and humiliation. Likewise, the deepest causes of healing involve the opposite: feeling honored, feeling valued, finding meaning in community. Frankly, I have been astonished on numerous occasions to discover how easy it is for the use of basic positive emotions, such as concern for family, love of friendship, respect for the dead, and above all, honor, to quickly transform a relationship between supposed sworn enemies.

I have come to realize that the only path toward a lasting solution for destructive conflict lies in a process of self-examination and spiritual growth. This is as true for those living in Jerusalem or Gaza City as it is for those facing a destructive conflict with a family member or former friend at work or in one's community. This path of true healing is demanding, but it offers us a sense of freedom and a way to recapture our energy. It offers us a way to realign our priorities as we move forward toward our best selves.

It is not difficult to recognize a destructive conflict in our own lives. Here are some of the typical characteristics:

- All of the obvious solutions are completely unacceptable for one party or the other.
- The participants feel that even if the original point of contention were solved, the bitterness and anger would remain.
- The conflict seems to have a life of its own, continuing

on and on in a cycle, despite the adversaries complaining about it and saying they wish it were over.

- There are signs that the conflict is not really even about the stated point of contention.
- The adversaries lose perspective and dedicate more time to the conflict than is justified.
- One or both of the adversaries may say they feel certain emotions—grief, disappointment, dissatisfaction—while it is obvious that other, stronger emotions are involved: rage, the desire for revenge.
- Both parties feel a desperate need to "win" the conflict because they feel their lives or their identities are at stake (even if this claim is not justified by external facts).
- The parties seem drawn to the fighting as if it is feeding or sustaining them in some way.

Solving destructive conflicts is by no means impossible, but a solution that breaks the deadlock requires at least some participants to undergo a process of transformation and healing, and the conflict itself will not be "solved" for everyone until all commit to managing the conflict in a more constructive way. Nevertheless, our own transformation is inherently beneficial to ourselves and to the situation. Realizing this, I decided that it was important to develop a set of guidelines to help people in conflict get to the bottom of their conflicted relationships and move from destructive emotions to the positive, healing emotions. These guidelines are encapsulated in the Eight Steps.

In *Healing the Heart of Conflict* I focus not on "resolving" conflict, but, as the title suggests, on healing it at the deepest level. Over a period of weeks and months, the process I teach can have an astonishing, transformative effect. As the examples I provide from my international peace work illustrate, the healing lessons of the Eight Steps transcend barriers of race, gender, politics, and nationality and can therefore be applied creatively to many destructive conflicts around the world.

The first eight chapters of the book, then, set out the path I recommend—taking the necessary steps to untangle the web of destructive conflict that can capture and immobilize us. Each chapter contains anecdotes from my professional work and the personal lives of myself and others, as well as references to philosophy, the great religious traditions, literature, psychology, the social sciences, and the latest techniques being used in international negotiations.

Unlike those who propose that conflict should always be addressed through talking, I believe the process of healing must begin with self-examination and *end* with extensive communication and dialogue. The Eight Steps, which I believe work best when followed in sequential order, ask us to do the following: Be, Feel, Understand, Hear, See, Imagine, Do, and then, Speak. The steps are deeply related to each other; each step prepares carefully for the revolutionary possibilities of what we can accomplish with the next step. The steps show us how to examine our inner lives so that our character becomes a true ally of healing. This leads us to pay close attention to the power of our emotions and those of others to heal conflict. We then understand the dynamics of what is really going on between adversaries, allowing us to listen to others in utterly new ways and with a new set of skills. Then we see revealing aspects of the conflict that no one else usually sees, and we start to imagine creative solutions that no one else dared see. All of this leads to taking powerful action that completely transforms hopeless situations. Finally, we speak in a way that uses the power of the word not to injure but to heal and create new realities. The key is that each step builds upon the strengths and abilities acquired by going through the previous steps.

In Part Two of the book we will apply what we have learned in the Eight Steps to the settings in which we most often encounter destructive conflict: at work and at home. Chapters Nine and Ten address destructive conflicts that can occur in our everyday lives and show how the Steps apply in each case. The final chapter, Harmonize, encourages us to take the lessons of the Eight Steps into our communities to make them happier and healthier. Chapter Eleven includes revealing examples from places of devastating conflict, such as Liberia, but it also discusses ways to make local community governments, small businesses, nonprofits, or any other organizations function in a harmonious way that brings the aims of individuals and communities together for the common good.

By taking the journey outlined in this book, we will become better and happier human beings because we will discover ways to restore broken relationships and build new personal and professional connections that are solid and deep. Too often we can become mired in the troubles of our personal and family histories, resigned to the fact that we are fated to endless conflicts in our families and our professions. We assume a world that must be conflict ridden. But through our steady progress we will come to see that whether in family, in friendships, in business, or in community, we can heal our conflicts and create a better world around us.

When I was young, no one made a career out of solving conflict or healing the wounds of war, but I have lived long enough to see thousands of brave people across the world now make conflict into a field of inquiry, a profession, and a professional passion directed at humanity's betterment. I was lucky enough that, just in time for me, society made some professional space for my deepest aspirations. I have been given the privilege of using my mind and heart on a daily basis to heal the wounds of violence, hatred, and fighting. My deepest hope is that those who read this book will discover the joy of healing the wounds of conflict and bringing happiness to themselves and to others.

PART ONE

THE
EIGHT
STEPS

CHAPTER ONE

STEP ONE: BE

Identity and Character

Who we are as individuals has everything to do with how we get along with others. Step One prompts us to ask ourselves, "What inside of me is contributing to this conflict, and what do I have to gain from it?" Being able to see yourself as you are can be the most important step in facing the damage that's been done as well as the damage that can be *un-*done inside of us all. This step is not easy, and yet it contains the most promise for leading us away from suffering and toward happiness. Even if this is the only step you take, you will surely be on the road to healing at least the conflict within yourself.

> **BE**: TO EXAMINE THE DEEPEST ROOTS OF CONFLICT WITHIN OURSELVES AND MAKE OUR OWN PERSONALITIES INTO AN ESSENTIAL AID IN HEALING CONFLICTS.

The beauty of the Eight Steps, however, is that one naturally leads to the next. Once you see what role you play in perpetuating a difficult situation, that knowledge will change your attitude toward others, which in turn can begin the healing. Many people go through their whole lives suffering in conflict, not knowing why. Just looking into the mirror will lead to surprising growth.

Terry Smith felt that her colleagues at work had been avoiding her for months and, the more she thought about it, maybe even years. This weighed on her not only as a baffling aspect of her professional life but also at the basic level of her personal identity. She had given up family for career, and yet a career without respectful colleagues can feel like no career at all. Terry felt assaulted by lower-level workers seeking her help for one thing or another while neither the powerful partners in the firm nor her peers included her in the really big projects.

From what Terry said, it did seem that some people were avoiding her. And so she went on day after day feeling like a victim. But *her* version was not the full story. Terry had a habit of taking on more work than she could handle. She was so insecure that she said yes to every project. She tried to insert herself into everything because otherwise she felt she would not be where the action was. In so doing, she was failing badly at the basic requirements for becoming a permanent partner in her firm. She left projects half finished and then covered up her failings or blamed them on others. She would complain loudly about the burden under which she worked, but then when others would leave her alone to complete the work she would cry foul and claim exclusion. This behavior made her unreliable, but also dangerous to be around. Her internal conflict had caused her to lose the trust of her colleagues. To repair the damage done to her professional career as well to regain a sense of personal happiness, Terry needed to examine her own character.

Self-Examination as a Start

Often we will become "attached" to a particular conflict or even to a series of conflicts as the way to be in the world. This hard reality may run completely against our intuition; we tend to think of conflict as happening *to* us, not something we encourage. In the heat of a destructive conflict the very idea that we might need to examine our own motives seems ridiculous, insulting, wrong; it seems like that's blaming the victim—us. But acknowledging our own role is the first and most important step in order to prepare the way for a clearer understanding of our conflicts.

Self-examination yields insights about what is going on inside us at any given moment and how it subtly but decisively can lead to conflict. Consider what I call the spiral of anger. This spiral commonly begins when one person does something relatively minor to hurt another, provoking a reaction that notches up subsequent responses to a more hurtful level until there is a full-blown breakdown in relations. Let's look at this phenomenon in the context of a typical day, during which, for most of us, there are many stressors and many opportunities to get sucked into such a spiral.

Sara rolls out of bed in the morning and heads straight for the bathroom scale, where she sees that she's gained two pounds literally overnight. She feels frustrated as she thinks back to what she ate yesterday. She curses her genes, which she blames for her difficulty in losing weight, but deep down she is also angry and disappointed with herself.

She proceeds to her daughter's room to wake her up for school. Sara is already in a frustrated state, and so when she discovers that her daughter is sneezing uncontrollably, seemingly in the grips of an allergy attack, Sara reacts to the situation rather than remaining centered in herself. Now she is feeling impatient with her daughter as well as with herself. Sara's self-directed anger has spiraled into the family sphere.

Then Sara goes downstairs to the kitchen and over her morning coffee hears about yet another terrorist attack on the radio. Her children see her reacting to the news and sense the tension she's experiencing even before she's dressed for work. The result of this spiral of anger is a bad start to the day for everyone.

Now let's look at the opposite, what I call the spiral of resilience that can spin things in the opposite direction. Like many people, I have some difficulty confronting people with whom I am upset. My little daughter has no such inhibition. She'll telephone a friend who has been ignoring her in school and state exactly how she is feeling. She listens while also pointing out why she is hurt. They settle matters in a couple of minutes! I stand aghast and impressed by the speed and ease of her engagement. In a moment my seven year old has displayed more negotiation skills than my wife and I could have hoped for.

Similarly, self-examination led six important political leaders of the latter half of the twentieth century to take immense risks with their careers and even their lives. They did it in order to save millions of human beings from war and endless conflict: Anwar Sadat of Egypt, Yitshak Rabin of Israel, Mikhael Gorbachev of the Soviet Union, F. W. de Klerk of South Africa, and Nelson Mandela, also of South Africa.

President Sadat made an unprecedented peace offer to Israel that resulted in the historic Camp David Accords, the first accords in history between an Arab Islamic country and the state of Israel. Sadat began the process with his daring visit to Jerusalem and to Israel's Parliament on November 7, 1977. This set off condemnation of Sadat throughout the Arab world, and eventually he was assassinated by Islamic radicals. Sadat was greatly admired by President Jimmy Carter. In a speech before the People's Assembly of Egypt on March 10, 1979, Carter said, "I feel admiration for the land of Egypt, and I feel a profound respect for the people of Egypt and for your leader, President Sadat, who has reached out his strong hand to alter the very course of history. . . . Sixteen months ago, one man—Anwar el-Sadat—rose up and said, 'Enough of war. It is time for peace.' The extraordinary journey of President Sadat to Jerusalem began the process which has brought me here today. Your president has demonstrated the power of human courage and human vision to create hope where there had been only despair."

Some years later, Israeli prime minister Yitshak Rabin made an unprecedented series of official overtures to the Palestinian leadership as he initiated a process of official negotiations between the Israeli and Palestinian peoples. He, too, was severely condemned by Jewish extremists. He, too, was assassinated. On the last night of his life he went to a peace rally attended by tens of thousands in support of the negotiations. Friends say that on that night he was truly happy.

In 1993, F. W. de Klerk and Nelson Mandela shared the Nobel Peace Prize "for their work for the peaceful termination of the apartheid regime, and for laying the foundations for a new democratic South Africa." Both leaders avoided what could have easily been yet another African tragedy of genocide and ethnic warfare. De Klerk was branded as a traitor by many in the white community who felt that he was putting their entire future at risk. The threat of personal harm was certainly real, as he, too, could have been killed by extremists. Further, his historic move toward power-sharing would not benefit de Klerk personally, as there was no way that after more than a century of repression black Africans would turn to a white man for leadership. Mandela, too, took grave risks preaching on the one hand reconciliation and on the other amnesty for so many criminals of the apartheid era.

Mikhael Gorbachev, likewise, paved the way for the end of both the Soviet Empire and the Cold War. For this he was popular in the West but not at home, and he lost power rather quickly. The Soviet Union could have limped along decades longer, brutally suppressing efforts to break it up. There could have been numerous wars with breakaway states, and one shudders to think about what could have happened to the USSR's vast arsenal of nuclear weapons in the wrong hands. Everyone knew that by opening up the Soviet Union to change, Gorbachev could also open up a floodgate of disintegration. The Russian state was a fragile amalgam of many different nationalities artificially forced together, but any move to shrink it or even suggest that possibility must have felt to millions of proud Soviets like a threat to their very existence. In the hands of leaders of less vision, the Soviet Union could have engaged in countless wars of enforced unification, not just one war in Chechnya.

Together, these courageous leaders took a stand for peace and saved millions of lives. They did not do what was politically expedient; instead they did something that is astonishing and all too rare in human history—they risked their political careers and indeed their lives for the sake of what was right and what was needed. These men were not paragons of self-examination at every moment. They were just as prone to impetuous, thoughtless behavior as the rest of us. Yet at a critical moment of their mature lives they asked the truly important questions of themselves, and the answers they came back with gave them wisdom and the courage of their convictions.

There have been endless studies on the political and economic circumstances that led to these fateful choices, but most overlook the fact that these men made choices inside their hearts. Their decision to take an active and honest role in ending complicated conflicts entailed intensely personal self-examination. They asked themselves the kinds of questions that ultimately all of us should ask: about the meaning of our lives, about what we are willing to sacrifice and even die for, and about the legacy we leave behind. These are the indispensable questions of being.

In the examples I've given, I've tried to show the personal, the familial, and the international ramifications of understanding and facing our anger. We have but to see how anger can affect human relations, and how real healing can be accomplished, to learn how to address conflict in our own lives. And it all starts with intensive self-examination and observation—with learning how to *be* with ourselves.

Self-Examination as a Spiritual Journey

It is human nature to be only partially conscious of what really moves us to act. Again and again in difficult situations we find ourselves reacting in ways that surprise us, sometimes positively and sometimes negatively. And so we grow by learning from our experiences, by looking at how we live. The examined life is one in which we are always checking ourselves, acutely aware of what is happening to us right here, right now, on this day, at this moment. By being in the moment like this we can gain important perspective on all aspects of our lives. Further, a heightened sense of being is conducive to avoiding destructive conflict so that we can concentrate on the truly important issues of who we want to be, now and in the future, as family members, as friends, as productive citizens, and as leaders.

Developing the capacity for self-examination has been a goal of many spiritual traditions. One of the Eightfold Paths in Buddhism, for example, is Right Understanding. In Judaism, *behinat ha-nefesh,* examination of the soul, is a critical component of moral growth, characterized often as a long-term or lifelong process of *teshuvah,* repentance, or more literally, turning toward or returning to one's Creator. Confession in the Catholic tradition and discernment in the Mennonite and Quaker traditions also entail careful examination of both our inner lives and outer responses to the world around us. In confronting our inner lives, we may face such unpleasant sensations as loneliness, frustration, anger, jealousy, and impatience. Rather than suppressing these things, we get to know them well and even treat them as old friends. Even if we see these traits in sharp contrast to our better selves, it is important to know our enemies, to know all their little tricks, in order to overcome them. An old rabbinic adage from the first century teaches, "Who is a true hero? He who can make an enemy into a friend." If we become friendly with the more destructive side of our inner lives, we learn how to neutralize its worst effects.

Taking up Terry's case as an example again, she had to face up to her good qualities as well as those qualities that were alienating her from others. She needed to see the complicated way in which her best impulses, such as agreeing eagerly to every project in order to please everyone, actually led her down a path of anger, alienation, and poor performance. Sometimes people like Terry cannot see their own negative role in any way, but I have found that the more supportive, the more private, and the safer the environment is in which they are exploring these painful matters, the more likely that my conversations with them will combine seamlessly with their own self-examination. This is especially true when I combine that process with a great many compliments because at the very moment that all of us are forced to face something negative about ourselves, that is precisely when we need the most support from appreciative friends. Only then can we discover honesty. Honesty in self-examination is like a powerful medicine, but it cannot be ingested without a great deal of sweetness.

Self-Care

In order to engage a path of self-examination, especially in the midst of tough conflicts, we must prepare ourselves. We must engage in a great deal of self-care and even self-love. Being honest with ourselves is not about shattering our sense of self or blaming all conflicts on ourselves. Excessive self-blame is especially dangerous for women who, in many cultures, are conditioned to take on blame in a conflict situation. On the contrary, it is about embracing who we are completely and seeing the best in ourselves in order to admit to the problems we have.

I have conducted numerous training programs for students of conflict resolution over the years. I remember Stacy, a wonderful student from England who wept uncontrollably when there were any difficult moments in the one weeklong conflict-resolution training program that I was conducting. As difficult as the sessions could be emotionally, I sensed that something else was wrong. It eventually emerged that Stacy and another woman in the class had both experienced either spousal or sexual abuse and were deeply wounded. The other woman, Nita, was unnaturally silent in class, more so than anyone else.

It became apparent that neither woman had the courage to confront her inner conflict, and that any difficult encounter resulted in a self-inflicted shutting down through weeping in one case and in the other case, silence. They were hurting themselves because they could not benefit from the give-and-take of conversation, role-playing, and other aspects of the training. They needed to unmask the damaged aspects of themselves in order to flourish more fully in social settings. Their negotiation of moments of conflict needed to be less focused on blaming themselves and more on the problems they saw in others.

Stacy and Nita had exactly the opposite problem as Terry! If they could avoid internalizing the conflict and inflicting hurt on themselves, they could become better equipped for later stages of healing conflict, such as listening and speaking effectively. They could not do this until they stopped blaming themselves.

I had intense encounters with Stacy, and she wept through most of them. Since then she has written to me that she is doing fabulously well in her life. When she came to my class what she was ostensibly looking for were skills to help others with conflicts. What she needed to do first, and in fact what she did finally do in that fateful week of training, was the healing work of caring about herself.

A Capacity for Humility

What we learn from both Stacy and Terry's cases is that sometimes we need to appreciate how really wounded we are and how much we have to heal ourselves in order to move on in healing conflicts with others. But sometimes people have the opposite challenge: They need to stop blaming everyone else for a moment, take a hard look at what they are being accused of by others, and consider how subtle habits of their own attitudes and behaviors set in motion bad relations with others.

Facing this challenge takes an important moral quality— humility. The people who negotiate conflicts the best are people who have an ability to poke fun at themselves without falling apart. The humility derives from an inner strength of character, not weakness. That strength is ultimately disarming in dealing with potential friends and even adversaries.

Millions of people around the world have an abiding respect for the Dalai Lama of Tibet. He is revered by millions as a leader of his religious faith, Buddhism, but also because he is fighting against the repression of occupation under which his people have lived for more than half a century. Many have died or been tortured, especially fellow monks. The situation has improved over time for Tibetans inside the country, but the Dalai Lama remains in exile, as does Tibet's original government and tens of thousands of other Tibetans. The Chinese Communist government continues to transfer thousands of Han Chinese citizens into the land of Tibet, hoping to destroy any hope for the reconstitution of the Tibetan people inside their land.

The Dalai Lama is an amazingly engaging speaker and a prolific writer, but it is his charm that is so captivating. A critical component of that charm, and one of the reasons we tend to believe what he says, is his capacity for humility. There is hardly a major talk that he delivers where he does not poke fun at something about himself or his Buddhist community, or in which he does not engage in mischievous behavior that makes light of his personal dignity.

I will never forget the day that I appeared on a panel with him. Thousands of people from every walk of life were in the audience. The Dalai Lama comes with a large entourage, including a translator, but he seemed frustrated that day by the translator. He wanted one, but he very badly wanted to communicate directly in English. He had just switched to the translator, but as the translator was translating, the Dalai Lama bent down to the floor and started playing with a child near his feet. We did not know what to do—watch him distracted on the floor, or listen to his words only then being translated. Around that time, the Dalai Lama had been quoted as saying, "Enough with all the chanting!" Now, chanting is an important part of Tibetan spirituality, and he was not implying that they get rid of it. But he was ready to take a look at himself and raise questions about how he has spent half of his life as a monk. By playing with children while speaking to us he was above all being himself. Everyone attending the panel learned a profound lesson that day.

The Dalai Lama gains many allies in his struggle for justice this way. Without a single soldier in his army he has gained the support of people from around the world—rich and poor, famous and anonymous—due to his extraordinary character. Fortunately it has become difficult for the Chinese government to kill him or crush his cause with such a following.

A key component of the Dalai Lama's character is a unmistakable generosity toward his adversaries. When you can see and admit faults in yourself it is also easier to be charitable to your adversaries. It is easier to give them the benefit of the doubt, to try to see the best in them, even as you oppose the cruel things that they have done. When we think of how the Dalai Lama does this we have to see him as the representative of his people in confrontation with the people of China. The most frequent excuse for Chinese brutality against Tibet and prejudice against its people has been that they are seen as backward. That is exactly why the Dalai Lama tirelessly engages Western science, for example, in order to teach his people a new way of being in the world. In this way he models how he as a leader and representative has to own up to the imperfections of Tibet's culture and past. In doing so, he clearly hopes that the Chinese will have the courage to do the same.

To be both self-confident and self-critical challenges all adversaries to do the same, to copy your behavior and respond in kind. If they refuse to respond in kind, however, the dignity and generosity of your behavior is endearing to bystanders and onlookers, which strengthens you in your just struggle.

So far the Dalai Lama has not been able to move the Chinese leadership into a constructive relationship with the Tibetan people, although things have improved considerably since the dark days of China's Cultural Revolution during the late 1960s. It is estimated that more than eleven million people died across China, most of the monasteries of Tibet were destroyed, and thousands of monks were murdered by Chinese Red Guards. Nevertheless, the Dalai Lama's inner skills have strengthened his position and his people's destiny. He is a model of someone whose very being can confront destructive conflict in a powerful way. With every new book he writes that exudes a confident—but not arrogant—wisdom, with every new overture to the Chinese leaders, he is doing what he can to keep the conflict between Tibet and China to legitimate issues that should eventually be subject to reasonable negotiation and compromise. He has resisted personalizing the conflict or using it as an opportunity for violence. He could have easily done so. He lost everything at the hands of the Chinese, lost many of his monks to brutal murder, and almost lost his own life as he escaped. But his nonviolent approach leaves the door always open for even his worst enemies. Under the extreme situation that exists between the Tibetan people and the Chinese government, it is doubtful that any leader could have kept his people as safe and as hopeful as the Dalai Lama has.

Courage to Acknowledge

Humility also implies the capacity to say and believe the words "I do not know the answer to that." This statement implies an openness to discovering paths forward that you have not thought of or that may be the opposite of what you had planned. This openness is critical in conflict situations. When you are arguing for a position in negotiations, who are you going to believe, the person who fights every single point and always must be right or the person who can distinguish between his own mistakes and other important issues?

For example, I am not inclined to trust the Chinese government that denied for months in 2003 that there was a

SARS epidemic until it had gotten out of control. It was revealed that Chinese officials actually hid cases from international inspectors. This deception did a great disservice to all the decent Chinese doctors who were working feverishly to contain the epidemic, and it endangered lives around the world.

This trait of knowing when you don't know all the facts or understand all the conflicting feelings involved in a conflict is another aspect of being honest with yourself. It involves what is commonly called a reality check. It's important to reflect on how much you are pursuing some conflict because of the right and wrong of a certain situation and how much you are determined to satisfy your own ego. Practice in and concentration on humility gives a person flexibility and is central to being a good healer of one's own conflicts and those of others. It requires allowing for other interpretations of your own values. The vast majority of our conflicts are not over differing values but over differing interpretations of shared values. Learning to live with others who have different interpretations of the same values is one of the key goals on the path to being.

Two parents love their children and think that making financial sacrifices for them is difficult but essential to their happiness. They share values such as a strong belief in the advantage of a good education and a healthy lifestyle. Their son, Max, is a bright child who is stimulated when exploring new talents, but he does not thrive in classrooms. Max also needs to exercise to be physically stronger. He loves swimming and he loves chess, and he has an opportunity to pursue one or the other of these activities, but not both. Both options are expensive. Father gets behind swimming because he remembers how debilitating it is to be considered a weakling. Mother knows how difficult it is in life to be taken seriously intellectually, and so she leans toward chess. The parents fight over which activity Max should pursue, chess or swimming.

It would certainly help them get past the conflict if they were able to see how their own, personal experiences influenced their choices for their children. They both need to watch carefully—as all parents do—when they are projecting their own needs onto their children. This first step, being, suggests that they step back for a moment from their own viewpoints and openly acknowledge their most cherished shared value—namely, their love and care for Max's future. They could say to themselves, "Wait a second. I know we both want the same thing here: a happy, healthy kid with a bright future. Am I so sure that my suggestion is the only one that will accomplish this goal of ours? Maybe my spouse is right. If we just discuss this together, maybe we can figure out how to achieve both goals over the long term."

Some conflicts are between right and wrong, better and worse, but most are not. Most are self-righteous struggles over good, shared values. But when no one is listening to anyone else, perspective is lost. Humility gives us the space to examine what values we may in fact share with our adversary in order to approach a situation in a more constructive way.

Finding Meaning in Conflict

Another major cause of conflict is something that, in principle, should be a positive endeavor: the search for meaning in life. Unfortunately, sometimes people decide that fighting can provide such meaning. This outlook is most tempting when family or business relationships become confused or when lives have been shattered by changes in fortune. "I can't be the owner of my own business the way I thought I could. I am going on fifty now, and I will never have enough spare capital. But I am sure as hell going to get back at that S.O.B. who refused to give me a simple loan. I don't care how rich he is or how smart he thinks he is. He stiffed me. He ruined my chances at a decent life, and I am going to let everyone know who he really is." "Mom is never going to treat me with the respect I deserve, no matter what I do. But I sure don't have to put up with that sad excuse for a stepfather that she has thrust into our lives." I have also experienced this kind of thinking in communities that have been devastated by decades of violence. "Everyone in my family has either been killed or hopelessly impoverished by *them*. I will not stop until I have driven them out of this region. I did not know what to do with my life until now. Now I know that those pigs are to blame for these hardships. I have finally figured out that *this* is the fight that is worth living and dying for. I will be the stuff of legends; my father would have expected nothing less."

Shifting ourselves and our adversaries away from fighting requires discovery of a meaningful way to exist in relation to others that does not require conflict, anger, or hatred. Just getting ourselves to look in the mirror and face what conflict does for us is half the battle in altering our style of interaction with others. Only then can we begin to search for new ways to find meaning without violence or endless conflict.

It may be human nature to sit back and recognize *in others* that conflict is ruining their personalities and their options in life, but conflict is more insidious than that. What we should be looking for is not what it does *to* others, or what it does *to* us, but rather what it does *for* us and for others. Looking from that vantage point will put us in a much better position to undermine conflict's addictive quality.

Attachment to destructive conflict as a part of one's identity often has tragic consequences. I remember interviewing someone once, we will call him Steve, who was so embedded in war with another group that he was talking seriously about the need to assassinate his own leader, who was about to compromise with the other side. He and I were sitting under some trees, relaxing over lunch. He subtly broached the subject in a way that would test my response. He said, "I don't know. Something has to be done about him. Maybe somebody has to do something." Less than a year later, that leader, Yitshak Rabin, was dead.

My startled reaction to what Steve said is exactly the reason why we end up understanding so little about people and why so many interventions are a waste of time. We avoid the really deep places of rage, preferring instead to talk to more "civilized" folks. What we really need to do is probe further at these rare moments, ask more questions, and listen deeply. We need to probe ourselves just as much for the quiet places of rage and attachment to destructive solutions to our problems.

When I probed Steve about his beliefs, his justification shocked me in its candor. He did not know who he would be without this war. He had sacrificed decades of his life to his nationalist cause, and decades cannot be retrieved. He did not even know why he would remain a citizen of his country if he could not fight. "Why not go and be rich in America?" he said. What he was fighting for was an ethnically pure country with which he could completely identify. Steve became the country and the country became him. If his country were to be at peace and become an equal, truly multicultural society, then he believed it would become just another materialistic country and he would become just another barren capitalist with no sense of meaning and no unique identity.

I had to contain my revulsion and see Steve as he saw himself. I believe that Steve was on a journey of meaning; he was looking to escape materialism in his own life. He wanted something more, and he found that not inside himself or in his own lifestyle, where it would have been healthy. Rather, he found meaning in ultranationalism, in an overidentification with race and group superiority.

The search for meaning is resolved for many of us

through our bonding to something larger than ourselves, such as the care of and love for children or a country, a large clan, or a religion. This bonding gets tricky, however, because in Steve's case he expected his country to be exactly what he dreamed it would be, an ethnically pure state, in order for him to be *personally* fulfilled. It is not the search for meaning that is inherently unhealthy, but the discovery of meaning through social oppression and violence.

Many people hold onto a conflict as if they were holding on for dear life. They change their lives and their identities so much for the sake of conflict that they do not know who they are or what to do with themselves without it. They have become the conflict.

Mourning Old Identities as a Way Forward

If you recognize just a little of yourself so far, then you are on the right track toward self-examination, toward being. If you also recognize an adversary, or a family member, or a coworker, then in taking this step for yourself, you may end up having a powerful influence on those around you.

In later chapters we will examine other alternatives to this attachment to conflict, and all the steps combined are designed explicitly to give meaning to life without destructive conflict. Here are some initial recommendations based on *being*.

A key to healing the heart of conflict is facing head-on the fact that you need a change in your identity, an identity that you treasure. Sometimes you can take advantage of abrupt shifts in circumstances to create a change in identity and sources of meaning in your life. And you must mourn over that lost identity. Mourning is a powerful way in which we shift identity. When I have mourned in the past over lost relatives and teachers, for example, I distinctly remember also mourning over the loss of who I was in relation to them, the dependence that I developed on those relationships. Sometimes an entire meaning system for my life depended on a loved one's life. Mourning signals the end, the wrenching process of purging that old personal identity, making way eventually for a new one. It can take years, and that is fine, as long as the path is being taken.

Alan Crenshaw is a thoughtful religious leader from Northern Ireland with a reputation in his community for honesty and integrity. As the Peace Accords of 1998 were beginning to have a positive impact on relations between Catholics and Protestants in 2000, I received a call from Alan. I did not know him, but he had read my first book, in which I have a portion on mourning the past, and he was eager to ask my advice. Alan proceeded to ask me an astonishing question: "Can you help me figure out a way for my community to mourn over this [the peace process] in a way that will not be destructive? We don't know who we are going to be without this [the Protestant/Catholic conflict]." For me, standing outside the Northern Irish/Ulster conflict, I was elated by news of progress. I thought that anyone and everyone would be relieved by the end of violence and the beginning of a peace process. It never occurred to me that peace could evoke mourning, but Alan was extremely perceptive.

It is true that I had written about the need for enemies to mourn their dead and mourn each other's dead as a way to reconcile. But it never occurred to me, until Alan posed the question, that people need to mourn their past identity in order to build a new one with a new way of discovering a meaningful life.

Alan sensed a kind of mourning already underway in his people, but he wisely saw that such mourning can either be constructive or destructive. It can lead to violent expressions of anger, or it can lead to the discovery of a new identity and new meaning. It would depend, at least in some measure, on his leadership, on other leaders, and ultimately on the choices inside everyone's hearts.

We talked about ritual, and about learning from how we mourn the dead—celebrating their good points and trying to move people on in their lives, focusing them on the reasons they have to live.

What if the people in that congregation didn't have someone like Alan? Other leaders might let them live in denial, the way human beings do when they cannot face the fact that a loved one has died. They pretend everything is the same politically in Northern Ireland, and yet reality creeps in and assaults their stability and sanity.

Hypothetically speaking, these folks, without Alan's guidance, might lash out in rage when reality hits, such as when someone from the other group moves in next door or when their own child ends up playing with a child from the other group in school. They might take the law into their own hands with threats and assaults, even against little children who are attempting to go to an integrated school. Some people actually did this in Northern Ireland, and their reactions outraged the world, and yet they could not understand everyone's outrage at their behavior.

Such folks are determined to renew the war because they are completely ill-equipped for a new identity and path of meaning. They do not know who they are in the present because they only know who they are in the romantic past. They have not mourned their dead or the death of their old war-based identity. Denial is a natural stage of grief, but when people stay in that stage they often end up acting self-destructively.

Alan Crenshaw is a wise man, and we have to consider ourselves fortunate that there are leaders like him in Northern Ireland. He has taught us that wherever possible, and as soon as possible, we must express grief over our conflict and the way in which it has fed our lives. We must actively pursue mourning in order to embark upon a new path of spiritual and personal meaning.

Defining Ourselves in New Ways

Another challenge of examining our being is facing the fact that sometimes we come to define ourselves against another person. It seems unavoidable in certain circumstances. This relationship may become the basis of our identity and a way to distinguish between good and evil in the world. For example, maybe you were not sure who you really wanted to be in sixth grade, what kind of role you wanted to play in your class or in the schoolyard. But then one day you saw two older kids picking on a weaker kid. Maybe that day you stood up to the bullies, and that action became part of your identity. Life is filled with opportunities for us to define ourselves this way, and there is no shortage of criminals at home and abroad that serve nicely as a foil for everything we consider evil in the world. Since our own sense of self is always evolving, it is easy to succumb to this way of defining ourselves.

What we do or don't do so often defines us, to ourselves and to others. President George W. Bush said in a number of speeches in 2001 that he was not sure how his presidency would be defined, what legacy he would leave, but the war on terror and terrorists—for better or for worse—would answer this question for him. On the other hand, self-definition is a tricky thing. If you define yourself by war, if it is your legacy, then military options can easily become your only solution to complex problems, and it will always narrow your set of options as to what is the best and most right thing to be done.

It does often seem to be the case that we need to define ourselves against something. The question remains how we can do this without falling into the trap of negative or destructive self-definitions that only lead to perpetual conflicts with others. There is a common expression, "Hate the sin, not the sinner." This expression has its origins in both Jewish and Christian religious sources from about the same period of the first century of the Common Era. The New Testament cites this idea, and in the Jewish rabbinic literature it is taught by way of story.

Rabbi Meir, one of the most brilliant and influential rabbis of the first century, was regularly assaulted on the roads by robbers. Rabbi Meir used to pray to God that the robbers should die, but his wife, Beruriah, a controversial and powerful woman of the Talmudic period, rebuked him. She cited a verse from the Bible and interpreted it in such a way as to express hope for *sins* to cease from this world, rather than *sinners*. The story continues that Rabbi Meir then prayed for the *sins* of the robbers to cease and then they stopped attacking him.

Religious stories from thousands of years ago can be quite cryptic, and we therefore may interpret them as simply miraculous cases of divine intervention. But I think that this story is trying to teach us to confront destructive behavior in the world from a healing perspective. Though it illustrates a way to eliminate destructive behavior, it can be seen as recommending an approach that does not abandon people, even those who are trying to hurt us in some way.

Coming back to our own conflicts, the implicit lesson is that if a recurring problem in our lives has formed an essential part of our identity, then let it be focused on conflict with particular things in the world that we resist or oppose rather than be fixated on other human beings. By fixating on the wrongs that we oppose, we do not abandon people but leave the door open to transforming bad relationships or helping others change in a positive way. If, for example, you are angry with your brother for how he has treated your parents, then be angry with the behavior, not your brother. Understand him, even sympathize with him, but stand against the bad behavior. In that way you can maintain your identity, deal effectively with the conflict without damaging yourself with hatred, and also leave the door open to your adversary to improve his relationship with you.

Here then are the key suggestions of Step One: Make self-study or self-examination a regular part of your life, especially that part of your life that involves ongoing conflict. Every week take time out to imagine yourself like a book to be studied or a movie to be watched. Watch yourself in your relations, and take a good hard look.

Care for yourself when you are engaged in tough examinations. No matter how many relationships are in a mess, do not take all the blame on yourself. No matter who is telling you that you are no good, be careful to not internalize the anger in such a way that destroys your sense of self. Be kind to yourself regularly, even as you take a good hard look at your behavior. Treat yourself to the things you love, especially on the days dedicated to self-examination. Work on yourself in environments you love, such as at the beach, on top of a beautiful mountain, or right before dining on a fabulous set of spare ribs.

When you get into the details of your conflict, try to look at it through humble eyes. No matter how clear everything seems, keep in mind that no one, not even raving geniuses, is brilliant enough to stay objective about themselves. Accept the possibility that you may share more values with your adversaries than you realize and that you can build on that even as you disagree on the interpretation of those shared values.

Take the time every week to search for the fulfillment of meaning in your life in at least one way that does not involve any destructive conflicts. Try to steadily build that into a happier sense of self that does not need conflict to flourish.

STEP TWO: **F E E L**

*Emotions as the Heart
of Conflict and Peacemaking*

tep Two involves a deepening of the process of self-
examination to help us identify the emotions that lead
to the conflict or conflicts
in our lives. Now if you're involved in a painful situation, the
last thing you might be inclined
to do is to further engage and explore your own emotional life.
Your feelings may be so strong
that you can't imagine how experiencing even more feelings will
help the situation. And that's
where many people get stuck in
a conflict. Remarkably, I have

FEEL: TO IDENTIFY
AND CONFRONT THE
EMOTIONS AT THE HEART
OF OUR CONFLICTS,
BOTH POSITIVE ONES
AND NEGATIVE ONES,
AND THEN TURN THEM
INTO VEHICLES OF
GROWTH AND HEALING.

seen that by getting in touch with our deepest feelings we will
discover a reservoir of emotional strength within. Also, by
recognizing how our internal life connects with the wider
world, we can begin to identify and accept what others are

feeling, including those with whom we're in conflict, which can lead to healing.

Deep feeling involves not only positive and negative emotions but confusing contradictions. If you just disliked someone, you'd walk away. It is when you both love and hate someone at the same time that some of the most damaging conflicts occur. This chapter will help you sort out contradictory emotions and set the stage for the healing strategies to come.

Let's say, for argument's sake, that your boss takes away a project that you loved working on and gives it to a younger colleague. You don't know for sure why he did it, but you naturally build suspicions in your mind. Maybe the last thing you want to do is explore your hurt feelings. After all, acknowledging the humiliation feels like even more defeat, and you have to get up and go to work the next day. And yet you just might, through self-exploration, become a little less attached to the project and more caring of yourself. Maybe the age of the coworker who took the project bugs you because you are getting older and have not made peace with that. Maybe, truthfully, there were aspects of the project that you didn't feel entirely comfortable doing, and you look forward to beginning something new. Or, maybe you simply lost a political battle for the project, which happens all the time and to nearly everyone.

Reflecting on your feelings can lead to many interesting insights and new ways of coping. But suppose that instead you decide to swallow your hurt and forget the whole affair at work. The next day a coworker whom you consider a friend mentions the project and says, "Better luck next time." *Better luck next time?! Who the hell does he think he is?* Your "friend" has brought back all those feelings you ignored: losing the project, your wasted effort for two years, the whole ugly episode. Do you laugh nervously and slink away, embarrassed? Do you mumble angrily under your breath and stomp off? Or do you proceed to botch the relationship by offering a generous, "Screw you!" There's a good chance that your friend would have absolutely no clue why you said that or where it came from. All he wanted to do was try to express some degree of empathy. Now a tough situation is much worse because you did not take the time to feel, with all its challenges.

People have a tendency to deny destructive emotions such as rage or jealousy. It is difficult to admit these feelings because we are trained to think of them as unacceptable. Yet not acknowledging them leads to their persistence! This is equally true when it comes to dealing with communal and global conflicts. Those who try to fix conflicts, personal ones or global ones, should not see emotions as the enemy, something to be suppressed, managed, and purged, but rather as a potential ally.

By being aware of our feelings, we can learn about the deeper aspects of a conflict, and indeed about issues that affect the meaningfulness of our lives. Any good psychologist understands that radical emotions are an important window into the psyche, and therefore a golden opportunity to explore paths to healing. And yet, many lawyers and diplomats feel that emotions have no place at the table of human problem solving. That is precisely why I made feeling one of the first and primary steps of healing all human conflicts, from the personal to the global. Reverberations of this step will be felt in all subsequent steps.

Facing Contradictory Emotions

In order to live with extended conflicts, we often have to shut off many positive emotions that we have buried. We feel like shutting down love for a friend or spouse who has hurt us, for example, in order to resent them with gusto and lack of remorse. This is a basic defensive instinct against getting hurt, and it also helps us organize confusing situations that could paralyze us. At the moment of anger, in the heat of common conflict, it is as if there is a court inside your head and you are building a case against your adversary. The last thing you can afford to do is mention anything positive about the other person or group. Inside your head you are prosecutor, judge, and jury, and any positive feelings you may have for the other person or group is immediately silenced. *Irrelevant, your Honor!*

If you cut off bad emotions and don't face them, you can't help but also cut off good emotions. Good emotions such as love, romance, care, sympathy, respect, generosity, gratitude, forgiveness, and patience are essential to recovery, healing, and a new relationship with adversaries. Healthy emotions are what you want to engender in yourself, and, for true healing at the deepest level, they are what you ultimately want to evoke from your adversaries.

Professional mediators sometimes shy away from invoking feelings, believing that a "rational" result can be achieved only if we do not "indulge" feelings. Perhaps this may work in simple conflicts, but it is a recipe for superficial negotiation, stalemate, and destruction of relationships in most complex, long-standing conflicts. Understanding the complex mix of positive and negative emotions that we go through in difficult relationships, by contrast, will help to extract the good emotions and build on them.

I was struck by the relationship in the movie *Bounce* between Gwyneth Paltrow and Ben Affleck. Paltrow plays a young widow who lost her husband in an airplane crash. Her husband was not supposed to be on that flight, but Affleck, who had just met the husband in an airport bar, traded tickets with him. Affleck had a connection to an airline worker who made the ticket switch, and Affleck wanted to stay overnight to have an affair with a stewardess. He is then plagued with contradictory emotions over the crash. Affleck struggles to cope with feelings of relief at being alive as well as feelings of utter guilt.

Affleck meets Paltrow, who plays the widow, and is taken with her. He never says a word to her about her dead husband. He wants to be honest with her but something holds him back. He is falling in love with her, and she is with him, and he lets the relationship go on unable at every turn to tell her the truth. He is living out a strange fantasy of comforting the wife, replacing the husband, and confronting the shallowness of his previous existence—all at the same time.

Paltrow's role is more straightforward: a grieving wife who hates that people feel sorry for her but in reality is vulnerable and lonely. Affleck, on the other hand, is dealing with a whole complex set of emotions that lead him to do something destructive: he conceals vital truths. He loves her and yet cannot face her anger should she discover the truth. The lie gets bigger and more damaging, the drama builds, and Affleck's character waits for a crisis to occur to force the issue. I will not spoil the ending for those who have not seen it, but *Bounce* has a Hollywood ending. Real life is more risky.

It would be far better for Affleck's character to have examined his simultaneous love for Paltrow and revulsion at the death of the husband and his connection to that death. He risked the entire relationship by denying the complexity of what was going on inside him, and he ended up hurting a grieving widow terribly. Many women would have walked away from him at that point. That is what *feeling* is designed to avoid: the web of tragic behavior that often results from unexamined complex emotions.

The writers accurately assume that most of us live like Affleck does in the film, shifting confusedly from one moment of relationship in our lives to the next moment, hoping that everything confusing will somehow get fixed. We vaguely hope that our contradictory feelings will work themselves out somehow. This unconscious way of living is dangerous for human relations. When we don't really know how we feel, our actions are directed sometimes one way, sometimes another. Far more constructive is to extract the positive and constructive feelings from a situation and then build on them to create relationships of greater and greater clarity.

Positive Emotions That Rescue Relationships

Isaac and Ahmed were partners in a difficult enterprise of fostering better relations between Israeli Arabs and Israeli Jews. I have had the privilege of observing and participating in their work, counseling them on expanding their base of support, and promoting their work where I can. They were intent on creating warmer relations between their two communities, despite enormous hostility and outstanding grievances. These two men had similar characteristics. Both greeted you with great affection, looking into your eyes. Both made you feel respected and warmly welcomed as soon as they met you. Both were profoundly religious.

They put their plans into action one evening by inviting forty people to a festive occasion at Ahmed's home. There were some dignitaries there, men and women representing a wide variety of religious and educational backgrounds. The evening had two components: one a gathering in the living room in which everyone was invited to speak and offer blessings and hopes for the future and the second a large, festive meal.

There were many beautiful and hopeful things said on

that occasion. One elderly gentleman, however, the most senior member of a nearby village, began to speak in the most bitter tones. He spoke about how his community had been injured and questioned the usefulness of "all this talk." I was keenly interested in what he had to say. Others became agitated, but we all listened to him for a long time without interruption.

The old man listed many grievances, all of them legitimate. There were many legitimate grievances on the other side as well. Usually such talk under different circumstances will lead to bitter debates, interruptions, shouts, and countershouts—but not here. *Why?* I wondered to myself. It was undoubtedly the effect of Isaac and Ahmed and several others who crafted the evening. They were not necessarily thrilled with the old man's soliloquy as it did not exactly fit the spirit of the evening, but it did bring the evening in direct contact with harsh realities that had to be faced.

The open atmosphere of the evening is what affected the old man, me, and everyone else. When someone is feeling respected, welcomed, honored even, then they are much more likely to feel like being generous in the emotional sense of the term, and generosity of spirit is critical to healing. Although the old man violated the intent of the meeting, it was manageable, even important, because the positive emotions at work in the atmosphere were so overwhelming. They overwhelmed you from the moment you were escorted to the home to the moment you left six hours later.

Feelings of warmth, welcome, hospitality, generosity,

and honor saved that encounter from the usual cycles of abuse to which people in both communities had become accustomed. Isaac and Ahmed have to work at this. It may come natural for them to engage these feelings themselves, but it is never easy to engage these feelings in others under less-than-ideal circumstances. This requires great discipline and commitment and, in particular, a strong mind and heart.

Some of Isaac's and Ahmed's friends are especially committed to the uses of joy and humor in breaking the boundaries that separate them from others, and I continue to marvel at these people. No matter how bad the situation, positive emotions are generated when they gather people and greet them. An emotion that seems to lie beneath joy and humor for them is courage. It takes courage to engage in humor in the midst of conflict, to express affection, and to honor people from a community that is against you.

Some will look at this behavior and say that they skirt the issues of conflict. They are so focused on the pleasantries of human relations that they do not get to the hard issues, but that is not true. What they do is set the stage for those issues by preparing everyone's hearts to hear these things. That is why the old man was listened to and why he was not shouted down by others.

It is true that some people cynically use polite dialogue to gloss over serious problems and that such dialogues can go on pointlessly for years without any serious change in relations or the situation. But there are many others in such conflicts who understand how to use dialogue wisely. They cultivate positive feelings in themselves and in others by using the moment of meeting between adversaries to take the tough steps of reforming actions and deeds that lead to a different and better reality.

In the hands of Isaac and Ahmed, the positive feelings generated in such meetings flow seamlessly into the step of imagining a solution, which we will address later on. It is a mark of great welcome to other human beings when you share your hopes and dreams with them and when you listen patiently to theirs. It is a kind of intimacy that allows the hard talk of problem solving to proceed in a better way.

I remember in a separate episode, when one of their more amazing friends, Gabi, was working with a different group. Again, despite all the laughter and friendship, some difficult issues came up. After the talking had gone on for a while and some points of disagreement seemed impossible to resolve, there was a lull in the conversation. Gabi then said with a big smile, "Friends! It looks like we have a lot of work to do! But I know we can do it." It was an infectious optimism that suggested a quiet confidence that these friends could work out a way to coexist.

There is no compromise without trust and respect, and being heard, being acknowledged and honored are critical to building trust and respect. The only danger is if such empathy is not followed up by the other steps to change the relationships and improve any conditions of unfairness. Then positive feelings in such meetings could appear as superficial window dressing. But these folks were far beyond superficial peacemaking. The friendship and devotion had entered into their hearts and clearly expressed to anyone who listened a long-term commitment to a better society.

The Transformative Power of Positive Emotions

There are other positive emotions that can play a vital role in healing conflicts. Seth is a fabulous businessman and community organizer in a small Ohio town. Seth has always had a wonderful way of making people around him feel good about themselves. From what I have observed, Seth has cultivated a lifelong habit of authentically appreciating everyone, always seeing the best in them. That is why so many people come to Seth for advice and everyone wants him on their side in a dispute. That has led to some challenges in his relationships, such as when a large dispute erupted in the town recently. He has his own opinions about who is right and who is wrong, but as a peacemaker what concerns him most is how to handle being continually pressured to take sides. I advised Seth to take a good look at himself and to acknowledge that he has become more important to his community than he may realize.

Seth has recently passed on some conflict-solving guidelines that he learned from a manual on community organization. But he continues to hide behind these guidelines and not assert his greatest strength, which is his own character. He suffers from some degree of underconfidence or overvaluation of others. The best way for him to move forward in his relationships is to build on his strengths, and that is his uncanny ability to make people feel appreciated and important. This will not immediately solve the larger dispute the community is facing, but it will maintain Seth's relationships, the trust he has built, and put him in a better position to help everyone involved in the conflict by steering clear of the partisan disputes.

Seth could also step back from "all these crazy people" and position himself inside a cold neutrality. This is tempting, it could work politically, and I certainly would be tempted to take that path if I were in his position. This would not help Seth build on his emotional strengths and skills, though, nor does it help the community.

I saw this same situation with Katrina, an amazingly talented archeologist who works at a prestigious institute. Katrina's discoveries in the field have given her great prominence at a relatively young age. Much is expected of her, and she is still feeling her way in her position of power.

Katrina has to face the personality limitations of those around her who are much more established but also frustrated by their lack of impact. Their lack of impact is often due to issues of poor character rather than professional talent; their colleagues simply don't like them or trust them. Katrina, by contrast, is loved by everyone—students, foundations, administrators—but this also puts her in a difficult position. The very characteristic that makes her beloved by so many becomes the object of jealousy by her older colleagues.

This kind of conflict is not limited to workplaces. It is

common in family hierarchies where younger siblings may, by virtue of birth order and family development, have skills not available to older ones, and the very characteristics that make them beloved to others make them the object of their siblings' jealousy.

Dealing with such jealousy is complicated to do emotionally. You don't want to deny or lessen the good traits you have, but you do want to manage the situation as well as you can, not allowing it to snowball into something negative. Katrina handles it by remaining subtly positive in all her relationships with colleagues. This is an emotional practice for her, a way of establishing her own space of confidence and care.

Katrina has come to create a framework of what I call porous boundaries. She engages others positively, always managing pleasantries, no matter how difficult her colleagues may be. On the other hand, she has clear boundaries inside of which she can be effective and powerful in her own work, and she will not surrender that space for the sake of keeping the peace with jealous colleagues. She has some pretty solid boundaries that prevent small-minded behavior of colleagues from getting her down or interfering with her work. She makes those boundaries pleasant, however, and most importantly, her boundaries remain porous. She is always open to colleagues who want to collaborate or evolve positively in their relationship to her, no matter what has happened before.

This recognition of her own space with porous boundaries allows Katrina to flourish as a professional inside a universe of her own accomplishments, a universe she shares with many admirers. At the same time, she leaves the door open at all times for difficult acquaintances and professionals to enter into a new relationship of collegiality and cooperation.

Let's say that instead Katrina tried to win over everybody who was jealous of her. The more she tries, the more her strategy misfires. The fact is that if she doesn't understand the feelings of jealousy as a normal response for others to have, then she is bound to invade the space of these colleagues who resent her already. She is killing them with kindness and stirring up even more ill will. Sometimes the best course is to make yourself available for relationships but not impose yourself on others. It takes wisdom and experimentation to know when others are waiting for you to make overtures and when your overtures are bordering on aggression. Katrina is wise, and that is why, on balance, most of the colleagues she interacts with admire her and care for her.

Finally, I want to highlight the power of feelings of unconditional care in emotionally tense situations. Maurice is a pediatric surgeon who is not especially famous. He is good at what he does, but he is not known for any groundbreaking procedures. Yet his office is continually overflowing with people who come to see him from around the world. Maurice is extremely skilled not only as a surgeon, but also at managing the emotions of his patients. I saw him one day interacting with children and their parents. What struck me was that most of Maurice's comments were not about the technical aspects of the surgery but about how to make the child feel comfortable. He held each one of the children. I even saw him diapering one of them and instructing the parents how to diaper while causing the least discomfort. His absolute love for children was palpable. The parents, in contrast, were full of nervous agitation, the kind that often leads to conflict. Maurice was completely disarming even while surrounded by that tension. This put the children in his presence at ease, and it put the parents at ease too, and that is the greatest gift he could give them at that difficult moment in their lives.

Maurice is wise as a doctor and a healer, but also as a strategist of conflict prevention. There is no potentially destructive conflict situation greater than when children are suffering. He taught me that the most powerful positive emotion that we can inject into potential conflict is absolute care. I have seen other pediatric specialists who also project so much care and even joy at seeing the children that you have to feel a greater state of ease in their presence. This allows everyone to calm down and concentrate on the important choices and paths of action.

Expressing absolute care is not appropriate in some conflicts, but wherever it can be applied, it should.

Balancing Emotions

We need to pay special attention to emotional extremes, in ourselves and in others. We may be too aggressive or not aggressive enough, too arrogant or underconfident, overly naïve or too jaded. We must examine all of our character traits and emotions to see whether they are currently functioning in a helpful or hurtful fashion. Emotional excess of all kinds leads to poor interactions with others and invites conflict.

Once we have identified any emotional extremes in our character, we should strive to bring them into balance. Such balance has been the goal of many of the greatest of philosophers, from Aristotle to Confucius, and thousands of their students throughout the past 2,500 years of human culture. In our modern society, here are some extremes to watch out for.

- An excessive emotional need to win in every situation, or its opposite, the fear of success. If we have an emotional block against success we can destroy a good situation or relationship in order to avoid it—and not even be aware that we are doing this. This trait is especially difficult to spot and often requires intense self-examination. The balanced perspective: feeling confident because of your own successes while at the same time welcoming and encouraging the success of others.
- The need to find an enemy, or its opposite extreme, the lack of courage to face a proven adversary. These opposing tendencies divide many nations into political camps between which there is no middle ground.
- Arrogance that disallows the possibility of admitting wrong versus excessive humility and self-blame to the

point of avoiding any kind of growth with others. The balanced perspective: enough humility to make space for others, as well as for one's own faults, but confidence enough to face difficult relationships head on. This applies to many family situations, where adult children need to be honest about their feelings concerning their parents.

• The need to be different from and seen as better than everyone else that expresses itself as self-righteous non-conformity versus the need to be so accepted that it buries personal conscience and the ability to stand alone for what is right. Balance entails combining the reasonable human need for social acceptance with an equally valid emotional need for uniqueness, for being somewhat different and special. The typical story is of the teenager who needs to express her independence, but it is also the case that some children are conventional to a fault, out of insecurity, and they clash with parents who they see as outrageous, society-defying, and embarrassing.

• Indifference or emotional distance that leads to misunderstanding a partner, family members, or especially a different point of view versus excessive empathy that leads to an over-attachment to one person in a conflict, say, one's child. A common example of this is the parent-teacher relationship, in which parents must support their children but also set a good example by respecting the authority and professional opinion of the child's teacher regarding academic performance and classroom behavior issues. Two extremes here would be indifference to your child's challenges at school versus the other extreme of being so moved by your child's pain that you lash out against the teacher, setting a bad example for your child.

• Bluntness to such a degree that one becomes unable to negotiate the fine line between constructive and destructive criticism of others versus feigned pleasantries and outright deception in order to get through conflict, which can hinder the rise of any trusting relationships. The balance is found by cultivating enough honesty to constructively and compassionately engage others in difficult situations.

Some people have learned how to cope with a difficult life by being emotionally detached and suppressed. They are not motivated to solve the problems they have with important people in their lives, and they act as if they do not care. Indifference where it seems strangely out of place is the key characteristic here. The opposite of this is a passion so strong that it prevents a person from reflecting on his own conflicts or developing the patience to listen to others.

One family I know has spent years trying to help a wayward son who seems so laid-back, but the fact is he never seems motivated enough to engage with other family members; instead he appears to do what they want to please them but never comes to grips with his problems. The son is apathetic and without goals, and he walks around most of the time in a gloomy state. Often young people will go through periods when they are figuring out who they want to be, but this boy was lost in this process for a very long time and seemed unhappy. He hid behind emotional distance rather than confront his parents with some pretty strong emotions he had about what he perceived as excessive control of his life. It was important in his case to express some of those emotions and start moving his relationships and his identity forward rather than remaining frozen in indifference. The indifference may have been his way of avoiding saying hard things to parents that he loved, but whatever the motivation, it was becoming far too costly to both himself and his parents. Sometimes the turmoil of tough emotional exchanges and negative passions can unstick a frozen relationship or a frozen identity.

The balance we want to strike is having enough positive passion to pursue reconciliation with others while being prepared for the negative passions that will be evoked by working out difficult problems, passions such as fear, anger, jealousy, frustration, and regret. Of course, these and other extremes of feeling will occur naturally at different times and under certain circumstances, but in general our emotions require a constant balancing act. We need to develop trust in the rhythm of the emotional roller coaster that is human life. We need the courage to be emotionally alive and not shield ourselves perpetually with the armor of feigned indifference. We need to believe that despite the power that negative emotions can exert over our lives, there is also a reservoir of positive human emotions that, when properly balanced, can help us heal and avoid damaging conflict in the first place. Being aware of the need for this balance is half the battle toward achieving and maintaining it.

Emotions at the Heart of Healing

Finally, what follows is a personal story of a relationship that has angered me at times but has also taught me about the central role of feelings in healing conflicts. If such a complex emotional partnership can survive, then surely there is hope for many other kinds of relationships.

Ryan has worked tirelessly on relationships between enemy groups for the better part of the last forty years. His stellar and courageous ways of creating relationships between adversaries immediately attracted my interest. We have worked together in an international organization that has over a period of decades come to specialize in developing friendships between members of groups that are at war with each other. Over a ten-year period he and I have periodically taken trips to various parts of the world as part of our work on healing conflict, particularly in Israel and Palestine. At times we have held different views about what should be done politically in the Middle East or about where the greatest share of blame lies for continuing violence. In a few difficult situations we faced intense conflict over what to do, conflict that turned out to be based on emotions from our past rather than the issues of the present.

I remember one trip in which we were engaged as a two-man team in a series of challenging meetings up and down the entire region. Each meeting was powerful and draining. We also had to deal with ever-changing lodging and travel arrangements. Driving in foreign countries is always a tricky affair, but in an environment of great conflict and occasional violence it can get seriously nerve-racking, at least for me.

We found that we were becoming angrier and angrier at each other for the silliest things, and it did not make sense because back home we were such good friends. It was interfering with our work in some ways, but as I felt the emotions and studied them I started to sense that our fighting also seemed to be a part of the odyssey that we were on. We are both emotional men, and quite strong-willed, but that did not explain the depth of anger that was occasionally erupting. I truly did not understand my own behavior or his.

People who study conflict have come to realize that complete neutrality is extremely difficult—if not impossible—to maintain. We all have biases that encourage us to favor one side or the other in any given conflict. I remember one night we were traveling in the West Bank, where Palestinians predominate. It was actually a time of relative peace, but periodically Jewish civilians had been abducted or killed in terrorist attacks. Nevertheless, we were there visiting Palestinians precisely because we both wanted to pursue friendship—a key method of our work—and to demonstrate our care for their situation.

It was dark that night and the roads were awful, broken and confusing, and there were few street lights. We got lost trying to find someone's house. As soon as the car went over the line to the West Bank, my adrenaline shot up and I was on high alert. I realized too late that driving at night in these circumstances put me over the top. That night I became convinced that I was in mortal danger. The darkness and the foreignness of the place no doubt contributed to this feeling.

Ryan was driving, which didn't help. I must emphasize as his friend that he is an excellent navigator, whereas I am amazed that I am able to get around my hometown. On the other hand, Ryan drives too fast. I don't know what had my blood pressure up more that night, the fact that we were lost in a potentially hostile area or Ryan's driving.

Ryan pulled over to ask some young men in a kiosk for directions. I remember their dark silhouettes, though I could not make out their faces. They were young Palestinian men, and all I could think about was that they were about the average age of the men and women who volunteer for suicide bombings. I was nervous and said to Ryan, "I'm not sure that is a good idea. . . ." He answered in his classic way: "Why not, they seem like good guys!" I was drenched in sweat in the car, in fear, as Ryan asked the men for directions and we went on our way.

Our meeting was uneventful, but afterward I told Ryan that I would never work with him again, that he had acted in a completely unprofessional manner. These are powerful words and strong accusations, and, understandably, Ryan became angry and accused me of an unprofessional bias against the Palestinians and a desire to undermine his work for peace.

After a day, I realized that my relationship with Ryan and our ability to work as a team was more important than anything that had happened during our drive through the West Bank. I began to examine my own behavior and realized the extent to which I had been influenced by extreme emotions. I certainly had reason to be nervous, as a rabbi, traveling in the West Bank with no protection. But I had no reason to accuse Ryan of unprofessionalism for asking for directions when we were lost. We were simply in different emotional states and that affected our calculations of proper or acceptable procedure.

Fortunately, I later asked Ryan if we could talk honestly about our feelings. I explained my fear and tried to convey to him what it was like for me to travel on a dark night, lost, in a place where religious Jews just like me had been abducted and murdered. I explained that many of the terrorists who attack Israel seem like nice, ordinary people when they are arrested or when, after a suicide attack, researchers try to understand what motivated their actions. Ryan needed to hear from me what I was going through more than once because the psychology of it was so foreign to him. The more I explained it to him, oddly enough, the more I began to understand the feelings myself. In the end, Ryan forgave my outburst and in addition became much more sensitive to the issues I might face traveling in Palestinian territory. I, in turn, came to realize how unfair it was for me to attack him.

There is an ironic end to this story. On a completely different night, also dark and full of mishaps, Ryan and I were traveling to a remote Jewish neighborhood of ultra-Orthodox Jewish Hasidim, who wear black garb from Eastern Europe. I was paying a visit on a sect with which my ancestors had been affiliated not long ago. For me it was an interesting and emotional reunion that served, in addition, as an opportunity to explore the full spectrum of points of view in Israel about war and peace.

As I look back on the incident I realize that Ryan was not comfortable with going there, though he said nothing to me. We got out of the car and Ryan locked the keys inside by accident. I had the appointment and had to go inside while Ryan stayed with the car and waited for assistance from the rental car company.

Just about then the Hasidim were gathering for evening prayers in a hall near where the car was parked. A Hasidic man approached Ryan and motioned for him to come in. He refused despite the fact that it was cold outside. Eventually Ryan realized that the Hasidic man simply wanted to offer him a cup of tea.

When Ryan told me the story later, it became obvious that Ryan was terrified of these Hasidim. He said something to the effect that he did not know what these men would do to him as a non-Jew. Now whatever else you can say about ultra-Orthodox Hasidim, they do not go around attacking non-Jews. There are some thugs among them who have at-tacked Jewish Sabbath breakers, and some who have attacked Jewish women who were scantily clad, but certainly in gen-eral they do not set out to harass Gentiles.

Ryan later admitted to me that he felt alienated when-ever we met with groups of ultra-Orthodox Jews and that he felt judged as a non-Jewish person by people with such a strong faith. Ryan described how their strange black garb put him on edge. The ultra-Orthodox man outside the syna-gogue, near Ryan's car, went out of his way to persuade Ryan to come in for a cup of tea, but his only agenda was com-passion for a stranger.

Ryan and I have seen how strong emotions affect our judgments in conflict, but we also recognize that it is our emotional bond that has kept us together as friends and part-ners, through thick and thin, all these years. We are reminded that emotions are at the center of all the relationships that we cultivate. Sometimes they are problematic, while other times they result in healing. Ultimately, though, there is no real progress in human relationships without emotions at the center.

CHAPTER THREE

STEP THREE: UNDERSTAND

Knowing Your Conflicts

One of the great advantages of the human capacity for communicating with others is that we can benefit from the collective experience and wisdom of all of humanity in dealing with conflict in our own lives. If we look at conflicts only through the lens of our own experience and our own emotions while ignoring how they are affecting others, our perception of what is really going on will be distorted. Such a selfish perspective cuts us off from feedback that we need to solve our own problems. So many others have taken journeys of healing before us, and their stories are told through great books, religious masterpieces, cinema, the experiences of friends and elders, to name just a few. Our understanding of others and their experience of conflict is the key to understanding ourselves.

UNDERSTAND: TO ESCAPE THE BOUNDARIES OF YOUR OWN PROBLEMS BY COMING TO KNOW OTHER CONFLICTS, AND TO TAKE FROM THAT KNOWLEDGE THE UNIVERSAL LESSONS OF WHAT WOUNDS AND WHAT HEALS.

The truly great forms of art take you on a journey of self-discovery. One such journey is recorded in Robert Redford's memorable film *The Horse Whisperer*. Redford plays a cowboy famous for taming and healing horses. His character, Tom Booker, hails from a line of men who are reputed to be able to calm a horse's wild rage. Booker lives on a magnificent ranch in Montana with his sister's family; he is middle-aged, divorced, without any children, and we come to know him as a lonely but confident man with enormous gifts.

In complete contrast to Booker stands the MacLean family from New York City, who are bedeviled by stress. Their daughter Grace, played brilliantly by Scarlett Johansson, is involved in a horrific horse-riding accident in which her dearest friend is killed, her own horse is badly damaged and insane with injury, and she herself loses a foot. Grace's scars run deep, and it is not clear that she can emerge from the darkness that envelops her. The film explores the many conflicts that must be attended to in order for the MacLean family to survive this terrible trauma. Grace has to imagine her future, and the mother has to decide who she really is as a wife and mother. The father remains in the background, rather patiently waiting to see the outcome of his wife's and his daughter's journey.

Grace's mother, Annie, played by Kristin Scott Thomas, is almost a caricature of a city dweller. She is an anxiety-ridden, hard-driving business executive who doesn't communicate effectively with her family even though she does love her daughter intensely. Annie has an iron will, and she determines that only Tom Booker can save her daughter emotionally by saving the horse at the same time. She takes her daughter and the horse on an audacious journey across the country to visit Booker at his ranch.

Booker's genius is that he perceives animal needs—and human needs—at a deep level, learning from virtually everything that he sees and hears, whereas the MacLeans are people who have trouble understanding themselves at the most basic level. Booker is a man who also knows his own needs and weak spots well, and that is all the more reason that his close bond with the mother and daughter, as well as with the horse, will be difficult for him. He reluctantly agrees to help the family out of empathy for the vulnerable and angry young girl. From there, things get complex emotionally for everyone, and the great drama of the film ensues.

There are various themes at work in this story: the love of children and the debilitating fears that grip parents, the way those fears eat away at the sanity and serenity of parents, the desire to live, the occasional desire of unhappy kids to die, the imprisoning effects of regret and survivor guilt after tragedy, anxiety about the future and about one's identity, and, last but not least, the search for courage and hope. It becomes clear as the plot develops that it is important for Grace to feel the emotions of her internal conflicts and her external struggles with her mother. When we first meet her, she hates everyone and everything. Her bitterness pervades her character, and if she isn't able to reflect on her feelings and how they will affect the rest of her life, those feelings will eventually kill her. The key for Grace, as well as for the rest of us, is to resist acting on the destructive feelings, or at least to learn to limit the ways that we do.

The farm, which is so breathtaking in its beauty that it has an almost spiritual quality to it, the healthy relations of everyone there, the incredible skills of Tom, all lead Grace and Annie to a place of greater reflection and understanding, almost despite themselves. Redford believes in the healing power of nature, and this theme seeps into many of his films. A compassionate and reflective approach to life is contagious in a certain way, and it is that contagion that we hope happens as we watch the story unfold.

Just as Tom's capacity for reflection and understanding spill over to Annie and Grace, so too can we practice understanding in a way that positively affects those around us. This is a critical but subtle strategy for moving all of our relationships in a better direction. In the movie, Booker reflects on a number of things that help him set his course of action. He sees that Annie belongs with her family, despite the fact that it would leave him alone once again. He sees that Grace's essential conflict is not about whether she can become a less cynical person, or even whether she wants to ride again, but whether she wants to live. He also sees, as did her mother, that the fate of the horse and of the girl are linked. Grace's horse, wounded and crazed with rage, is an outer manifestation of her own inner life, and only the healing of her horse will begin her own healing.

Assigning Blame

When we fight we tend to simplify what is going on. We resist getting too wrapped up in assigning blame fairly; it is easier to consider something all one person's or group's fault. There is guilt, and there is innocence, and never the twain shall meet.

This situation occurs often among children from divorced families. When someone is absent, such as a divorced parent, it is easy to blame them for everything. On the other hand, if a teen, for example, is having a hard time with the parent they live with who must set rules, they may idealize the absent parent and demonize the parent they see every day. I know families in which a divorced parent is blamed and used as a means for the other family members to avoid talking honestly and taking responsibility for their own actions, or resolving arguments between them. This oversimplification is a reaction to the emotional confusion of conflict.

Conflict is confusing precisely because in most situations there is *not* a perfectly clear way to assign blame. It is extremely difficult for even the most seasoned and moral judges to figure out who is more right in most situations—it depends on your point of view. Also, more often than not we are so distracted in conflict by the hurt of someone's assault on us that we cannot even begin to examine our own role in the conflict. We are too busy defending ourselves or preparing our own attack.

We do this to our political leaders as well, as we blame them for everything that is wrong with our country. It is true that politicians can make terrible choices and that many of them, for instance, are indebted to special interest groups, but the truth is that most of the bad things they acquiesce to are things that are the responsibility of all of us as citizens. We can lash out at this senator or that congressman and bemoan his ties to the oil industry, but I have only to look at my own car to see where responsibility lies. What our insatiable oil consumption does to the earth, what it has done to politics, and what it has done to impact the level of global violence is a problem for each and every one of us. This is an easy concept to understand but a difficult one to accept: Leaders often only do what we ourselves are guilty of even as we refuse to take responsibility for our actions.

How We Communicate

Often relationships fall apart and conflicts are made worse than they have to be, not because of what we say or what we are arguing about, but due to *how* we argue. Sometimes everyone knows that what you are saying is right, but if you go about it the wrong way, others will fight with you just in order to avoid rewarding your behavior. There is no doubt that how we communicate leads to greater or lesser understanding in a conflict. (We will address this theme extensively in Step Eight, Speak.)

Then there are times when the offenses that people

commit against one another seem to have no explanation other than the fact that two people, or groups of people, come from vastly different cultures or worldviews. Many fights are due to two or more completely different interpretations of the same events. Most of us today inherit a variety of cultural influences on our character, as well as our habits of interaction. Some people, for example, interpret silence as a sign of respect, whereas others interpret it as a sign of coldness. Some people consider the basic civil responses of "please" and "thank you" to be among the most important indicators of whether they can get along with you. Others attach little value to what they see as superficial civility. Some people welcome an open, direct conversation in public when there is an issue to debate, while others consider a public display to be humiliating and wonder why the other person could not have approached them privately first. These are just a few examples of the kinds of differences in values and styles of interaction that can affect understanding and divide people.

It is also true, however, that around the world people utilize cultural traditions to build bridges among adversaries. Recently I moved with my family into a neighborhood in the South (in the United States). I was born and bred in New England, where we are used to being independent, perhaps to a fault. I did not even know neighbors in Boston who lived across the street from me, on and off, for forty years. But that is the custom up there. The first week we were in our new house we received gifts from every neighbor, and not just store-bought gifts but homemade sweets. This thoughtfulness set the stage for a great deal of good will. Indeed, a problem came up the next week with an overhanging tree and I was motivated to fix the problem right away. Sometimes customs and cultures divide, sometimes they generate bonds, and it is up to us to be conscious of both dynamics.

Conflict as a Trap

Conflict often resembles a drama in which we feel compelled to play our part, even when somewhere inside of us we would rather escape from our role. This drama seems to control everyone, as if there were an invisible director and the players stay in character through the final scene. The good news is that once we get to know this play, it is possible for us to change the script to one of reconciliation.

I remember observing the director of a vocational school over a period of years. Steve was a brilliant man but highly volatile; he had a significant temper and an odd sense of humor. Many students lived in fear of him, and most of his peers resented his occasionally tyrannical behavior, and yet everyone was beholden to him for holding the school together.

I was impressed by how much Steve's behavior would change when he received a great deal of respect from certain people. Steve became—for lack of a better word—sane, also insightful and reasonable to deal with. What struck me was that somewhere along the difficult path of his life he had learned to deal with stress, opposition, and competition from peers by acting unpredictably, even insanely, as if he were grandstanding or showing off acting talents for a script that he found himself in. Steve was trapped inside a script of odd coping mechanisms, and it got him into trouble on many occasions. He managed to carve out a career for himself, but he was always embattled. Steve clearly had a decent side to him, but he needed to understand how his coping mechanisms were trapping him inside a bad script and change it to be who he really was.

A sense of injustice and unfairness is part and parcel of most conflict scripts. Sometimes a person's interpretation of justice and injustice seems absurd to us, especially when that person goes on to do outrageously unfair things. All the more reason why making the attempt to understand everyone's sense of justice and injustice is critical to moving forward in resolving a conflict.

The moral sense of fairness and unfairness should not be buried or set aside in order to solve our conflicts. Even if it is sometimes misdirected, it represents a basically good instinct that we need in order to live a decent life and help others to do the same. The appeal to ethics, to our sense of right and wrong, may provide the basis later for fair compromises on visions and needs that both we and our adversaries have.

This has been a particularly difficult but essential part of work I have done in the Middle East. I had to learn not to pass judgment too quickly, but also not to forget what was right. All sides, including intermediaries, cannot lose sight of a commitment to ethics, even when the rules need to bend a little to achieve settlements. Violent conflicts are dirty, and the path to their resolution can get dirty too. True healing comes with solutions that leave our basic sense of right and wrong intact and at least somewhat satisfied. This is true for our adversaries as well.

Given the complexity of life scripts that people write or follow, we know we cannot achieve a perfect understanding of any conflict. We can achieve some clarity, however—enough for us to find a path of healing and happiness.

Power, and the Imbalance of Power

There is much that we know about why conflicts happen and why they get resolved. Several branches of the social sciences have studied these matters, including the social science of conflict resolution, and I am proud to teach in an institute exclusively dedicated to this work. But often this wisdom is buried in complicated studies that are not widely accessible and that do not properly address the moment-to-moment challenges of human existence. Our understanding definitely can be enhanced by this body of knowledge; the more insights that we have in our mind as we go through the steps, the more likely we are to pick up on things that we may not have sensed otherwise. So, what follows is a distillation of some of the most important lessons that have been passed down and how they apply to the step of understanding.

One of the most famous rabbis who lived during the period when the Romans occupied Jerusalem was Rabbi Yohanan ben Zakai, who according to the sacred texts of Judaism was faced with an impossible choice in the year 70 of the Common Era. The Romans were in the process of quelling a Jewish rebellion against the Roman Empire; Jewish factions were seeking independence from Roman rule; and the Romans were determined to set an example of the consequences of the rebellion by destroying the infrastructure of Jewish culture. Rabbi Yohanan, along with many Jews, was quite opposed to the actions of extremist Jews who had waged a terror campaign against the Romans. According to legend, he pleaded with the Romans to stop their destruction. They gave him a choice: either Jerusalem's central Temple, the holiest site in Jerusalem, would be destroyed, or the educational center in Yavneh would be destroyed. Rabbi Yohanan chose to save Yavneh because he believed that stones could be refashioned into temples but that the destruction of the educational core of the people could be lost forever if the seminaries were destroyed and the rabbis were murdered.

Rabbi Yohanan was faced with an impossible choice. Nevertheless, in those terrible circumstances he chose to resist the extremist path. This put him into a position to save Judaism and Jewish culture from total destruction. Yohanan understood that we need to have a realistic view of power in conflict and we need to make sensible evaluations of power in order to minimize the destructiveness of conflict over the long term. He rescued a safe place of peace in which the

Jewish community could recover despite terrible loss, and, indeed, Yavneh became a crucial center of learning that prepared the way for Jewish survival through thousands of years. It became the base for generations of learning and transmission of vital traditions so strong that they would survive many more tragedies over the centuries.

Rabbi Yohanan faced issues of powerlessness in violent conflict, but power plays an important role in nonviolent conflicts that are more typical of our lives. For example, I once advised a religious organization on a college campus about issues of power sharing. There were three distinct denominations of one particular religion, and there were inherent differences of belief and practice that divided them. Now, if these folks had done things badly and the resources, such as space for programming or services, were not shared properly, then the ideological differences could have turned into overt war between the groups. Instead, the directors of programming made sure that all resources were shared equally and that there were ample opportunities for the groups to mix. The potential for conflict was always there because of religious differences, but extra care was taken so that those differences did not become power struggles over space and resources.

It is the absence of a good structure that often produces conflict, and that is exactly why the founding fathers of the United States made the social contract of Americans into an institutionalized structure of democratic governance. Institutions such as an independent judiciary, a balance of power between the branches of government, a bill of rights—all are meant to create structures that help manage normal human conflicts, balance power, and prevent conflicts from becoming destructive.

My colleagues and I, when engaged in conflict resolution training, begin the training with a shared covenant or social contract between the participants. People decide on rules that everyone agrees to follow, such as avoidance of personal insults, limits to speaking time, and so forth. These rules create a structure of human interaction that allows for better conversations and more profound relationship building between the participants. In effect, we model in our trainings how to improve relationships in society by creating a temporary society with a good social contract. Rules that are fair can be helpful in a society; rules that are unfair will always create conflict.

Needs and Interests

Another key to understanding the structure of human conflicts is identifying our most basic needs and interests. An ancient rabbinic legend tells the story of a Master Ukba, who was one of the greatest scholars of his generation. Master Ukba was committed to the laws governing the provision of charity, and he subscribed to the notion that charity given anonymously was the most honorable and the least injurious to the poor. He therefore scrupulously avoided contact with recipients of his charity, money that he used to leave in a small crevice for poor individuals to come along later and take out. This arrangement went on for a long time.

One day Master Ukba was walking with his wife and he put the charity in the same spot as always. What he did not know is that a poor person developed an urge to meet him face to face, and so this person surprised Master Ukba. Ukba was flustered, shocked, and promptly ran away, with his wife trailing behind him and the poor person chasing both of them! What a scene that must have been.

Legend has it that Master Ukba and his wife ducked into the corner of a wall. What they did not know was that this corner had just served as a fireplace recently swept of its coals. Now Master Ukba's feet were burning, but according to the legend, miraculously his wife's did not burn. This depressed him endlessly because, as a God-fearing man, he assumed that this was a sign from Heaven that his wife was more righteous than he. And so the rabbi asked his wife simply, "What do you do differently from me?" She answered with magnificent depth and clarity. "The poor come to my doorstep, I welcome them into the house, I discover what they need, I give it to them, and then I send them on their way."

I have thought about this old story for many years because it teaches me so many things about the problems and challenges of poverty relief, human relations, and conflict. Mrs. Ukba understood the importance of individual human needs. She understood that anonymous cash can be a cold way to help another human being, even though the sentiment of not embarrassing the poor is a good one. She understood the sacred possibilities of human encounter, listening, and learning what it is that someone truly needs, and that, indeed, their most important need may be to be listened to with honor, respect, and compassion.

Human beings have basic needs such as food, water, a sense of security, and space to live. But we also have a deep desire for more subtle needs to be met, like dignity, empowerment, identity, and meaning. Less acknowledged but most important is our need to identify with things beyond ourselves, things that will outlive us. This could include a commitment to children and grandchildren; identification with an idealistic cause, a nation, a movement, a religion, or a deity, or all of them at the same time. Amazingly, some human beings will sacrifice all other needs for only one overriding need, like the need to do honor to one's country or one's God.

One of the most important aspects of understanding is identifying the needs that drive us and that drive the ones with whom we are fighting, because when we are able to understand and name these needs, something remarkable happens. We start to find that we actually have some legitimate needs in common with those who are fighting with us, and we start to discover ways that both sides can get at least some of their healthy needs fulfilled.

Old Injuries

We always have to ask ourselves whether the conflict we are in resonates with something that has happened long ago. We need to examine the lives of our adversaries and ask the same question. This takes some degree of courage because it is much easier to keep repeating old injuries and old conflicts than it is to than face them. But unless they are dealt with directly, old injuries have a habit of causing conflict at some unexpected moment. Historical injuries such as Cromwell's destruction of Ireland, the displacement of families in Palestine during the creation of Israel, and the centuries-long legacy of brutal anti-Jewish prejudice and violence are of critical importance to some of our most difficult international conflicts. Likewise in the personal sphere, old injuries can cause conflict years later, as when a parent favored one sibling over others, even if only for a short time way back in the past.

I once had a part-time job that I had no time for; I was paid poorly, and the situation made it almost impossible for me to be successful. I was working out of a chaplain's office at a small college, and the student leader with whom I was working had a hard time with me—and I with him. We never fought outright, and I had assumed that we were getting along well enough until I discovered near the end of the year that he had lobbied to have me replaced. This hurt me tremendously, because even though I had put in relatively little effort and honestly could not figure out how to do the job well, I still felt that I had had a good relationship with the students. Years later I happened to bump into this person at a family celebration, and seeing him just made my blood boil. He was friendly to me, but of course he had always been friendly—that was the betrayal. I did not know how to respond to him, and I realized immediately that the whole episode was still with me, even though I thought I had forgotten about it. In this case I hadn't understood how deeply that betrayal had affected me.

Related to old injuries is the question of whether any of the people we are involved with have made a lifetime habit of repeating their conflicts. It may be difficult to break that pattern, no matter how reasonable our efforts to reconcile may be, unless the pattern is exposed and confronted. The same goes for our own tendencies. The moment we recognize that, one way or another, the debilitating conflict we are in right now has plagued us before, our strategy has to be heavily directed to our inner lives.

One family I know engaged in conflict much of the time, and a daughter, Rachel, was usually the peacemaker. In solving their pattern of conflict the family members realized that Rachel actually enjoyed her status as peacemaker and, therefore, from time to time subtly undercut attempts to end family conflicts. She could not let go of her positive role in dealing with conflict, and this she had to confront. Rachel's reaction is quite understandable, for we often grab on for dear life when we find a meaningful role in the midst of a confusing world. Sometimes those roles perpetuate our problems, however, and that has to be faced.

A critical moment of reflection along these lines came

to a five-year-old boy in my daughter's class who regularly hit the other kids or tormented them in some way. The teachers did what they could, but it seemed like an ingrained pattern. At the end of the year my daughter was moving on to a new school and the other kids were asked by the teacher to compose blessings for her. We hung them up in her bedroom and they helped her cope with the move.

I found the words of the children fascinating. Most of the blessings were typical for Jewish culture, such as wishes for long life and good health. Amazingly, this bully blessed my daughter with the wish that no one should bother her or hurt her in any way. When I read it and realized who it was, at first I was just stunned, but then I drew a few conclusions. One is a likelihood that he himself experienced some sort of torment on a regular basis, possibly from an older sibling, and that therefore he naturally thought of a blessing to avoid this. The other is that composing this blessing was a moment of truth for him, a time when he recognized his own behavior.

What struck me is that the teachers happened to have developed an activity, the blessings for a departing classmate, that induced self-reflection in five year olds about their deepest desires and wishes for what life should give them or should give anyone, and this may have provided even five year olds with an opportunity to reflect on who they really are, who they want to be, and what it is about life that they wish for or value the most. The moment of self-reflection is about confronting yourself and who it is that you want to be.

Such moments often lead to a sense of liberation, or at least an awareness of what the real problems are.

We carry old wounds that remain hidden until some event triggers them, and that is how many conflicts burst forth onto the scene. We must remember this as we face our conflicts and reflect, in every situation, on what exactly is new, what is old, and how we can utilize this knowledge to better manage the conflict.

Mixed Motives

Rarely do human beings (or nations, for that matter) do anything for one reason only. Naturally, when defending our own actions we will tend to cite only the most noble of our motivations. Now it is perfectly normal to have more than one motive to act, but the key to preventing conflicts is to clearly state both our idealistic motives and our needs. The same is true in global politics. Nothing is more damaging than covering up your country's interests and needs and cloaking them in righteousness. There were many international arguments for and against the war in Iraq, for example, but rarely were the business interests of the major and minor players explored in any great detail in public. It is clear that Saddam Hussein was a menacing character on the world stage, but it is also the case that Iraq is an oil-rich country, and this had to be a factor in the administration's arguments for and against the war. It would have been more helpful for France and Russia to acknowledge their interests in keeping

Saddam in power and United States's interests in removing him from power, for example, in addition to the moral arguments that were made. Acknowledging your interests and needs makes it easier for people to accept the fact that you may have some good intentions as well as personal interests. It's called full disclosure, and it builds trust. Honesty in this area may have led to more international cooperation regarding Iraqi reconstruction and a more balanced global effort to advance the interests of the Iraqi people. Setting such an example of honest debate would have significantly helped America's reputation and thereby also contributed to the global struggle against terrorism.

Another, more personal example of how easily misunderstandings can lead to conflict was when I went to Israel in 1983 to a place where Jews and Arabs lived together in one settlement. It was a liberal part of the country, and I had the opportunity to spend some time with an Arab writer and some of his friends. One day we were walking on the crest of a hill in their settlement, and down below we could see a Jewish kibbutz, a farming community. I asked Marwan, "If that land down there was where your village once was and you had weapons, would you fire on them if you could?" And he said, "Yes, if it was my land." This made me sad, but I was silent. I understood his sense of injustice, but that he would be willing to fire upon a community with families. . . .

Later on that night I found myself with a big crowd of Marwan's neighbors in his living room, all Arab. They seemed interested in me, and I took them seriously, considering everything they had to say as a vital part of my understanding the complex situation in that region. I listened to every word and asked many questions. They shared with me how much fear they experienced whenever a terrorist bomb went off in Israel, because if they were nearby they could be accused and suffer a terrible ordeal. Having just come from a weekend at a Jewish home in Jerusalem, I related to them the fear of a Jerusalem housewife who was not having her kitchen remodeled because she was afraid to be alone with Arab workers. She said that she feared being stabbed.

At this point Marwan's friends expressed surprise at the fact that Jewish Israelis would be afraid of them. It was literally unbelievable to them. "They [the Israelis] have the guns, why should they be afraid?" was the prevailing sentiment. But subsequent events have proven these fears—on both sides—to be well founded.

Returning to that special evening with those Arab men, I thought back to what Marwan had said. I chose my words carefully in order to challenge them with the same process of understanding that I myself was going through by learning from them. After the men laughed about Jewish Israelis being in fear of them, I said to Marwan, "You remember what you said to me on top of the hill earlier today? That you would shoot if you had the weapons? That is why they are afraid of you, and that is why they want to make sure that you never get any guns." Marwan and his friends were not conscious back in 1983 of the fear that they evoked from Israeli Jews, only the fear that *they* experienced. In the same way, many Israeli Jews found it difficult to imagine how fearful Arabs were of them. More importantly, Marwan was not facing his anger and desire for revenge that was right beneath the surface. This had to be done before there could be any discussion of whose fears were more legitimate or what justice would demand of him and his adversaries.

Understanding conflict is not just about figuring out our opponent's position. It can be helpful to speculate as to what our opponents "really want," what they are not saying, but we will only access the truth if we have a basic understanding of many factors in conflicts, including our own role. As a rule, we tend to underanalyze our own role and overanalyze the role of others, overattribute problems and motives to them and underattribute them to ourselves. True understanding resists this very human tendency.

Step Two asks us to become adept at facing everything we are feeling, and also what our adversaries are feeling. This step, Step Three, asks us to become adept as well at the many dynamics at work that propel human beings toward or away from conflict, toward or away from a happy life. This is essential to taking further steps toward relationship building. Marwan and his friends, for example, were honestly shocked that their adversaries—people who appeared to them to be invincible—were terrified of them. Only understanding, won in this instance through conversation, allowed that growth to occur.

To this day I am amazed at how often Palestinians are shocked by Israeli fears and vice versa. We build up images of each other in conflicts that are emotionless phantoms, artificial pictures that have no basis in reality, and this distorts all of our responses. The Eight Steps make it impossible to pretend that our own emotions or those of our adversaries do not exist. We must face the inner life of everyone in a conflict in order to arrive at later stages of wise observation, wise vision, wise speech, and wise action.

STEP FOUR: HEAR

The Art of Listening

In the first three steps what you really should be doing is indulging and examining your inner life. Now it's time to expand your world beyond yourself. In Step Three you attempted to understand what others were feeling, true. But in Step Four your understanding deepens and becomes more profound. To really hear someone else is to listen for everything that you can find in what they are saying to you, or what they're saying to others, that can clue you in to what's

HEAR: TO SKILLFULLY LISTEN TO EVERYTHING, EVERY CUE, THAT MAY HELP YOU ENTER INTO THE WORLD OF THOSE AROUND YOU, ESPECIALLY THOSE WHO ARE IN CONFLICT WITH YOU.

going on in their inner lives and how they perceive you. If you listen carefully, over time your strategies for healing conflict will become far more effective.

Mike, a successful business consultant, was brilliant at listening this way. He was especially good at analyzing the stock market, primarily because he listened to everything

anyone said about a company, from information about its officers to gossip about its corporate culture. It all went into his
evaluation of the health of the company, helping him distinguish good business opportunities from bad ones. He even
cited this skill when pitching his services to potential clients.

Mike and I met and used to chat often at the coffee-
house where I wrote this book. I remember Mike describing
how the owners of a certain start-up company contacted him
for advice and a consulting contract. They asked him to contribute to their business plan, which involved a three-way relationship involving him, them, and their technical workers.
Mike's technical background and his business background
made him well-suited for the job.

Mike realized, after listening intently to everyone, that
the owners of the company had not informed the workers of
basic facts about the company's future. In fact, they were
planning to fire this group of subcontracted workers before
they were required legally to pay them fully. Mike told them
that he could not work with them under these circumstances,
and they eventually parted on good terms. From experience
Mike knew that these owners, in addition to being unethical,
were heading toward an absurd and unnecessary conflict and
that their business was most likely headed for failure even
though their product was good.

Mike's listening skills have saved him time and money
and allowed him to adhere to his own standards of honesty
and open disclosure, thus helping him to avoid situations
that could bring on inner conflict. Mike does not solve all the

problems of every company he works with, but he does often prevent employers and workers from becoming embroiled in serious conflict.

Other approaches to handling the situation might have led to disaster. Let's imagine another Mike—Mike II we can call him—who is a savvy analyst of business plans in the technical field. He too is a sought-after consultant. But he is underconfident and therefore too eager to please clients. A group of men come to him with their new start-up and they have lots of money and ideas. He is so eager to play a part that he loses the capacity to listen and inquire carefully. He is blinded by the fear that he will never have access to such money again.

A year into the business relationship the money is rolling in, but then the owners suddenly fire the whole subcontracted staff before their payment is due. Mike is shocked and horrified. He is fine financially—they have already paid him for all of his work and want to keep him on as a consultant—but he is outraged by their behavior and says so, particularly because he played a linking role between the technical staff and the owners. Mike exchanges words with the owners, who then start vilifying Mike and blaming him for the crisis. The owners are also being sued for breach of contract, and Mike will be called in as a witness. The whole industry knows of the case, and it acts as a hot potato that cools any interest in Mike's consulting services. He also has to hire his own lawyer.

One bad event follows from another in this alternative

scenario with Mike II. It is all traceable to a lack of capacity for listening that, in turn, emerges out of a lack of strength, courage, and confidence.

Listening as an Aid to the Other Steps

Real hearing happens only when we have completed the first three steps:

- When we have started to understand and appreciate ourselves (Be)
- When we have acknowledged the full range of emotions at work inside of us (Feel)
- And when we have begun to search for and achieve a better understanding of human conflict as a whole, armed with a perpetual curiosity to understand more (Understand)

At the same time, listening is constantly helping us accomplish the previous steps. Thus, following all the steps is like engaging in a cycle that feeds itself. Each step further reinforces the growth achieved by earlier steps.

Much of what we have learned till now involves work on ourselves, but with this step we begin to focus on skills and moral qualities that will transform relationships at the moment of personal connection with others. The moment of interpersonal connection is laden with risk. We can do so much good and so much damage in a short time, and we should therefore be prepared for both the promise of moments to be seized and the peril of moments in which we can lose everything by what we say or do, by what we hear or don't hear, by what we are blind to or see.

Listening as Both a Skill and a Moral Quality

There are two ways to view the qualities involved in deep listening. We can see them as a set of skills, or we can see them as a set of moral qualities. We saw in previous chapters that Be involves an artful combination of humility and self-care, for example. Humility is certainly a moral quality, but it also can be seen as a skill if it leads to a successful style of negotiation with others. Self-care is certainly a life skill, but it is also a moral quality if you seeing loving yourself as a moral obligation, as many ethical systems do.

Other qualities such as empathy and respect are part and parcel of the skills of relationship building. Listening leads to empathy, and empathy is the key to devising solutions.

At times we must face the fact that there are many forces of history and civilization that are larger than any one of us, and well beyond our control. When you find yourself in group conflicts or wars that are larger than anything you can control, then little victories begin to matter a great deal. Listening that leads to empathy with just one adversary feels like a kind of victory. It is empowering and it makes one feel at home in the world despite adversity. This kind of control is critical to our health and happiness, and seizing these moments of interpersonal connection is liberating. It stands defiantly before the other challenges of complex conflict.

Saleh is a man who I came to love and admire, even though we met only a few times. He is a man of intense religious belief, and he immerses himself every day in meditations on love and healing. We did some extraordinary things together in order to stop the war in Israel and Palestine, but with few long-term results, as is the case with most political interventions. Conflicts involving millions of people take years and years to heal, and what we try to do necessarily involves many failures until one day there is success. That is why faith and hope are so important, and why listening is also an expression of the moral quality of patience. The patience required of endless listening in the midst of years of efforts to heal is what creates lasting bonds of friendship even in the midst of war.

I recall a few months back that I was distraught over Saleh's situation. He was a prisoner in his own village, unable to move due to curfews imposed by the Israelis but also under intense threat by extremists from his own culture. (Peacemakers get it from all sides.) Such a hopeful and happy man, Saleh had turned bitter for a time because of being imprisoned. I called him from Boston one day and we cried together on the phone for so long. There really was little to say, except I remember that he kept repeating a Hebrew expression, "Akhi, Akhi, Akhi," "My brother, my brother, my brother . . ."

Calling Saleh that day was one of the hardest things I would ever do because I simply had to listen to his cries and I felt utterly powerless to help him. Several people had begged me to do what I could for him, but nothing I tried worked. Thus we were left with listening and empathy. But, at the same time, I felt a kind of angry determination well up inside of me during that phone call, as if our very relationship was an act of defiance against the madness of war. That feeling or perception got me through and helped me cope.

Hearing What Is Not Said

As we move forward in understanding, practicing listening, we should acknowledge that a major goal is to hear what is *not* being said. There are many things meant but never said, often because they are too painful to say. For example, a little child can only rarely bring himself to say that he is disappointed in a parent, but, on the other hand, many positive things that you would expect to hear from the child are not forthcoming. You notice that one child says I love you all the time but the other one never says it unless prompted, and this way of hearing what is not being said becomes a clue to detecting other problems.

There are two choices once we believe that we have heard something that was not said explicitly, but both choices carry risks. We can confront someone with what we think is not being said, but the cost of this choice is that we may be violating a private space that should have been understood but not spoken. Whether this is the case will vary from culture to culture and even across genders. Some people welcome unmasking things and reaching for more honesty, whereas others resent it and wish that things were understood and not spoken. Women may be more prone to communicate openly about what they intuit is going on, whereas men may leave things unsaid and then get flustered or even offended when what is unspoken comes out in the open. In the final analysis you must judge for yourself and experiment with what is the right balance of listening, silence, and direct communication about what you think is not being said.

Another cost of jumping to conclusions about what is not said could be that by making bad assumptions, and therefore wrongly attributing things to someone, we may alienate them. People can take enormous insult when you read something that they never intended. The potential benefit of confrontation, however, is that, after some initial discomfort we could take the relationship much further and set the stage for healing the conflict. We could at least set the stage for developing new ideas on how to resolve the conflict.

The other choice is not to bring to the surface what we think is going on. Instead we could say things or do things that respond indirectly to this level of insight. Listening and then responding with great subtlety creates an interesting space in relationships for experimentation. We may set the stage then for some profound transformation of relationship. The cost of not bringing everything to the surface is that we could be wrong in what we thought we heard. Also, we could lose the opportunity for honest exchange, which is what may be called for.

For example, Adam insults Jim by blurting out at a business meeting with the bosses a cynical aside about a disaster that occurred with a device that was designed by Jim. True or not, it was a stupid comment to make in front of the bosses, and Adam is immediately sorry. He comes over to Jim after the meeting and sincerely says to him, "I am really sorry. It was a bad joke to make in front of the bosses." Jim pauses, and says, "Apology accepted." Adam senses, however, that the apology is not really accepted, and so Adam has a choice. He can rest on his laurels and say to himself, "I did apologize," or he can admit that the damage was done in public and, therefore, more will be required of him to demonstrate to Jim that he is sincerely sorry. So the next time there is a meeting with the bosses, Adam goes out of his way to make suggestions that he explicitly states are based on Jim's excellent research. Hearing what was unspoken leads to action. Adam knew that he had to follow up with words and gestures specifically targeted at healing the damage done.

Listening as the Key to Leadership

Benjamin, one of my congregants, was a vice president at a large company made up of several different divisions. He came to see me because the company was facing a serious crisis that he felt he could not resolve. As he sat in my office, Benjamin told me that during his entire tenure, the company had divided along many lines: between men and women, liberal and conservative, pro-management and anti-management, and different approaches to work. Each of the official divisions also competed internally against one another. The result of this competition was an organization at war with itself, in which each new hire had the potential to tip the balance of power between the divisions, between men and women, between those who supported management and those who were unhappy. It was a tense, divisive situation and Benjamin had found himself in the middle of it. His responsibility as general manager was to coordinate the budgets and activities of the different divisions.

One result of all this conflict was that Benjamin was questioning his ability to do his job. He had considered leaving but didn't want to be branded as a quitter. Besides, he genuinely wanted to figure out what was going on so he could become a better manager.

The conflict at the company had blown up when Benjamin had taken a long overseas work trip, and representatives from one division, in the course of negotiations with the vice presidents from the other divisions, managed to get something for themselves at the expense of the other divisions. The result was that the workers at the other divisions felt hopelessly disempowered.

In the past, Benjamin had made promises to each of the divisions to keep them all happy. It became obvious to all when Benjamin was away that these promises could not be kept in view of the limited resources available to the corporation. People began openly questioning his competence as a manager, and Benjamin noticed viscerally that he had lost the respect of his coworkers.

In the course of the friendship that I developed with Benjamin, I helped him think through some of his feelings and attitudes. Benjamin communicated to me his despair about the situation. He also realized that he was disturbed by conflicts because he hated direct confrontations. It was this avoidance of direct confrontation that was a clue for me. Benjamin told me he "solved" most problems through private negotiation with everyone—which is not bad in and of itself. As I raised some of the issues of Be, Benjamin realized that solving problems in an open, honest, and courageous way was difficult for him. He realized that his private negotiation was primarily a means to avoid conflict and fighting. Even more than that, Benjamin acknowledged that he enjoyed making everyone feel that he was really on their side because it gave him a sense of power. In the final analysis, his management style only served to increase everyone else's dependency on him, and it was bound to perpetuate problems more and more with each passing week.

To be honest, the problems of the office were beyond Benjamin's skills. They were embedded and long-standing, and to Benjamin's credit he at least succeeded in keeping a lid on them for a long time. But he was the only thing keeping everything together. There were no working relationships that could survive difficulties without Benjamin. In some space of Benjamin's inner life this made him feel important, even though he disliked the fact that relations were so bad. He needed to face head-on his need for importance and fulfill it in some more constructive way.

The problems became even worse a short time after these conversations when some valuable employees left; this negatively impacted the status of the company. The general dissatisfaction was exploited by at least one rather disgruntled senior employee, Arthur, who tried to create even more division and disunity by engaging in rather deceptive behavior, such as hiding employee applications for job advancement when he considered those employees to be enemies! His personality flaws and moral failings made the existing problems particularly acute.

Arthur's behavior was a trigger for a system of relationships that had gone bad, but focusing exclusively on Arthur—everyone's temptation—was a way of masking the broader issues at work regarding the systemic lack of trustworthy group relations. Arthur was the trigger because his behavior was particularly outrageous, and it was easy to fixate on him as the core of all the problems. The workers in this company needed a better relationship as a whole, and then they would be able to withstand Arthur's problems. Arthur's behavior was the straw that broke the camel's back, but a well-fitted camel would not be breaking in the first place.

Achieving a solution for the company required that everyone involved, not just Benjamin, go through the Eight Steps. The key step for them, however, was Hear. After we had discussed and understood the conflict, I told Benjamin he needed to stop, for a while, his previous practice of promising things to everyone in order to patch over company divisions. Instead, even though he did not like conflict and found this difficult, he needed to simply listen to what the employees had to say as a group. I suggested organized sessions in which all of the employees, senior and junior, who wanted to could come and frankly discuss their perceptions of the problem with Benjamin without having to fear that their jobs would be affected. I suggested to Benjamin the kind of leading questions he needed to ask in order to listen in a sympathetic way.

- "What gets you the most frustrated here, and how would you fix it?"
- "What is an example of a good day for you, or your best day?"
- "What is your ideal vision for the company and your role in it?"
- "Which relationship is causing you the most grief right now, and how would you fix it?"
- "What do you most want and need from me?"
- "What do you think I, as head of the company, should expect from you, and how can we work together to make that happen?"
- "Can you be specific about the behaviors that most offend you? Was there ever a time when the relationship was better, and what precipitated the change?"

- After letting an employee list all grievances against others: "What brings out the worst in you, and how can we work through that or get around it?"
- "What do you most want to hear from others or see others do in order to work better together, and what would you be prepared to say and do in return?"

Most important of all, however, was the task of making Benjamin less central to the process of healing and transforming relationships. I suggested more parties and gatherings in which people would have the time to talk to one another without Benjamin, not in some secretive or duplicitous way, but openly, as a part of the process of creating better relations between everyone. The employees needed to engage the stage of listening themselves, and as they started to listen to one another attentively, only then would the burden on Benjamin begin to lift. The employees would feel more empowered, more adult-like, and this, in turn, would help them behave more responsibly toward each other.

The result of this process was that Benjamin was able to clarify his role within the company, win back some of the respect he had lost, and create a more healthy and constructive decision-making process for his coworkers to enjoy.

What we can learn from Benjamin's case is that there is a fine line between leadership and infantilization. Poor leaders lead by making everyone into infants. But the more that people are treated like children, the more they behave like children and the less likely they are to be able to successfully negotiate conflict as it arises, which only leads to bigger conflicts down the line. On the contrary, a truly flourishing institution can develop if everyone's skills in conflict become more profound and more constructive. Great leaders lead while simultaneously making those they lead more powerful, and they do this with humility and with the wisdom gained through listening.

Listening as the Key to Understanding Human Needs

Unlike institutions and corporations, families and communities are designed, ideally at least, to protect and nurture children until they are ready to make their own choices. At every stage of development, a child's maturation requires her parents to let go a little, to let her embrace new skills and responsibilities. The boundaries of these stages can be confusing, so parents need to listen closely to what their children are saying and tailor their actions and reactions based on what they are hearing.

Of course, parenting isn't easy, and to a large extent we learn as we go along. It takes experience to learn the subtle differences between what children want and what they truly need. This involves knowing how to listen for what is not being said. The same is true of our immediate communities.

As a good leader, you learn to listen for the difference between what people say and what they are indicating they truly want from you. For example, sometimes an offensive set of words is really a cry for help, attention, respect, or care. One experience stands out in my memory from when I served as rabbi of a congregation. I always got along better with those congregants whose relationship to the synagogue was on the less ritualistic side; in other words, people who were less inclined to focus on ritual and more inclined to focus on their inner spiritual lives. These folks were my base of support, whereas the ones who identified with daily rituals tended to be men and women whose Judaism was more narrowly defined and less open to universal human problems. I was, at least in part, responsible for being alienated from this group because something inside me—from childhood, no doubt—made me fear and avoid them, and this caused problems.

I remember that several times I ran out right after ritually conducting the services, not staying with these men for breakfast. I stayed with them for breakfast just a few times, and once or twice I found myself within earshot of some pretty offensive comments about one ethnic group or another. I got the impression that they said those things in part because they were not terribly tolerant, but also in part to get my attention, which I was decidedly withholding from them. That was irresponsible of me as a rabbi.

The truth is that my relationship with this group was fixable. Their provocative comments were an admittedly awkward way of telling me that they wanted me to care for them, to take them seriously. They too wanted guidance and friendship, and my response was to avoid them like the plague. It was an immature response on my part, and it ended up helping neither them nor me. I simply was not listening to them because I heard only what confirmed my fear and anger.

Two senior congregants said wise things to me before I left that community. One said that the antipoverty work that I was about to pursue—and which I thought would free me from having to work with narrow-minded people—would perhaps end up the same way, and that I could not escape the core challenges of human conflict or the reality of gross human failings. He turned out to be right.

The other congregant said to me that she felt I would be able to handle these matters in a few years as I grew older, and that—to paraphrase her—"you will grow more patient with the human condition." It took me thirteen years, the death of my beloved father, and a great deal of painful experience, but in the end she too was right. I have learned that patience with humanity is not an important virtue, it is *the* virtue. I have also learned from many profound mistakes, and while I continue to make them, I have come to know when and where to anticipate them and how to prevent or correct them. That is an essential part of the journey of the Eight Steps.

Good Listening That Leads to Action

Years ago I had a colleague, Seth, with whom I had little conflict on the surface but who actively opposed my work in the context of an organization to which we both belonged. This was complicated work, but, put simply, Seth completely identified with one group in the conflict between India and Pakistan, was personally invested in that group, and did not want my work *between* the two groups to be given any kind of prominence in our organization. It is common in work of this kind that it is extremely hard for even the best of peacemakers to not become overly invested in one group.

This behavior hurt me and also thwarted some vital projects. Seth is a fabulous human being in many ways. He knew our relationship was in trouble, and he made a gesture to me by giving me a gift. Seth engaged in the Seventh Step of *Healing the Heart of Conflict,* to which we will turn soon. He took action and made a gesture to me that tried to reach beyond the obvious political differences we were having.

Seth and I had a meeting with several people days after he had given me the gift. I talked about my positions, and so did Seth. I grew used to looking intently into his eyes and listening to every word he said. He is a man of great subtlety, and careful attention to him gave me the way to understand the depths of our disagreements and why he so opposed at least some of my work. From his perspective he was pursuing a righteous path. Seth saw himself as repenting, in a real sense, for the mistakes of his nation, which had abused the group he is now defending.

Now I consider Seth's approach to these problems counterproductive and too one-sided, but I decided to honor him in many ways, to listen intently, and to agree with him wherever I thought I could. He, in turn, reciprocated with various gestures. On balance I would say that my strength in maintaining good relations with him was my listening and its effect on how I both disagreed with him and supported him when I could. Seth's strength was in the actions he took in the form of gestures of goodwill. They signified to me that we were in serious conflict over key issues but that this had nothing to do with his respect for me. He not only made gestures, but he made them clearly and unmistakably so that I could not retreat so easily into self-pity and counterattacks. It is so easy in conflict when someone opposes you in public to feel so humiliated or frustrated that you just want to delegitimate him in some way or call into question his character. But Seth would not let me get away with that by the way he focused the conflict on the issues while simultaneously making clear his respect for me.

Our conflicts were never solved because they involve differences in philosophies and priorities of right and wrong in one particular conflict in the world. Yet Seth and I, after various mistakes on both sides, practiced a combination of hearing and doing that led to a peaceful relationship and minimized the damaging effects of our disagreements to the organization to which we both belonged. I think that we both engaged in a great deal of self-examination as well. I sense to this day that, in a strange way, our conflict over the issues persisted but the conflict between us as human beings was healed.

I have come to realize over time that because both Seth and I were trying to practice, each in our own way, the steps of *Healing the Heart of Conflict,* we took what could have been a destructive conflict and turned it into a constructive conflict. It is constructive because the conflict was about objective problems in the world that have no easy solution and that we must continue to struggle with. In practicing the steps we made sure that these problems did not turn into something that was destructive to us personally, to organizations, or to the people we cared about and were trying to help.

Listening and Emotional Transformation

Like all of the Eight Steps, if fully explored and engaged, this one is challenging. It is about developing the emotional readiness to truly listen to difficult things that your adversary has to say—difficult, because the words are an assault on you, or they may be difficult because accepting another person's story requires feeling remorse for your own behavior or the behavior of people you love. That is why listening must be practiced in concert with feeling.

I once paid a visit to the home of a man who was a senior dignitary on the Palestinian side of the Israeli-Palestinian conflict; we will call him Farid. He had been a negotiator on various issues between the two sides, and in the privacy of his living room he confided in me that the most important thing that he was looking for was an assurance of dignity for him, for his family, and for the Palestinian people. If there were true dignity in the proceedings, and as part and parcel of the emerging relationships, then they would not fail and all other issues could be solved.

When I related this comment to a junior negotiator from the Israeli side who had negotiated with Farid, he could hardly believe it. He was shocked by the words from this person he thought he knew. First of all, the junior negotiator argued, their relationship *had* been one of dignity. Of course, that was the junior negotiator's perception! Second, he claimed that the negotiations were about other "complex, more important issues"—as if affronts to dignity were not the single greatest cause of many wars.

The emotional truth of the situation was that Farid sensed an imbalance in respect and equality. *That* to him was the greatest indicator of whether the true needs of the situation would ever be addressed. He was far less impressed with rational arguments and complex legal wrangling, even though he was a successful attorney. The junior negotiator, however, was not ready for the emotional challenge of truly listening, or for the changes that it brings about inside of you.

Farid and I, however, developed a warm relationship. The fact that he could confide in me embarrassing stories of indignity that his family experienced meant that he already trusted me enough to listen and truly hear what he was saying. I felt honored by that because trust is a rare gift that sometimes comes after good listening; it should be guarded like a treasure.

Farid also listened carefully to me about subtle and complex matters, assessments of various actors and cultural situations. I remember a reference he once made to his struggle as if it were mine as well. We were in his living room and he was sitting across from his wife. He immediately caught himself, however, remembering the boundary between us, and said, "Of course, you would disagree with that struggle." Looking at him intently, I immediately shot back, "I never disagreed with your struggle but with the *way* it was conducted, its violence against innocents." His eyes lit up and he shot a look toward his wife, as if I had proven a point of his in their personal debates about the use of violence. Farid listened to me and I listened to him, and in so doing we became more effective at discovering real answers to healing the conflict. We began to advocate not only for new negotiations but negotiations in an atmosphere of dignity.

Listening cemented a relationship that will always be good, despite the ongoing war. I call him from time to time, in the midst of continuing violence. There is little to say often, except expressions of solidarity and care. Sometimes, in the midst of wars, the cement you place around good relationships, and the memories that you keep inside from those encounters, are the sole sustaining lifeblood of hope in the future.

CHAPTER FIVE

STEP FIVE: SEE
The Art of Observation

At important moments of interpersonal encounter, hearing is not enough. Many if not most of the true facts of conflict, the true ravages of damaging relationships, are never spoken but can be seen in glances and averted eyes. Seeing is about utilizing that knowledge to plan a different set of interactions with others that will lead to greater harmony in our relationships. This entails learning many skills that come naturally to some of us and not to others, such as interpreting body language and facial expressions and studying environments for cues to social dynamics. The clue to seeing, really seeing others in relation to ourselves, is to act as if you've put the mute button on the TV. You can see the true relationship between husband and wife, the true hurt of a teenager in an interaction with a parent, without knowing

SEE: TO SKILLFULLY OBSERVE EVERYTHING, EVERY CUE, THAT MAY HELP YOU ENTER INTO THE WORLD OF THOSE AROUND YOU, ESPECIALLY THOSE WHO ARE IN CONFLICT WITH YOU.

what they're saying. You can see from across the room the look of humiliation on someone's face without having to know what was said to them. Seeing is about the challenge of detecting what is not spoken but what we need to understand about others with whom we are in conflict.

A couple of years ago I took my daughter to a day-care center where she was rather reluctant to go. She is particularly sensitive to fighting; she becomes transfixed by it when she sees it, even if she is not involved, and it seems to depress her, at least temporarily. Even another child crying seems to affect her profoundly. After some observation I started to notice the subtle impact among all children of other children's cries.

We were concerned about Ruthie's situation, not because we thought anything was wrong with her, but because she seemed to pick up at a rather young age all the subtle problems of whatever environment she was in. This sensitivity is not so unusual among children. One of the major mistakes that people often make in child rearing is that we assume that the inarticulate nature of such small children, as well as their basic inability to understand time and distance, is an indication that they do not know most of what is going on. On the contrary, they seem to understand subtle interpersonal problems and conflicts better than many adults who can remain oblivious to the dynamics of a situation.

As a way of further exploring the situation, I decided one day to watch the playground of the day-care center. The teachers were standing around in a group, not looking very happy, and the kids, as to be expected, were all over the place.

The boys were running around in a pack, and most of the girls were playing in small groups, but some were trying to play with the boys.

One boy was just crying uncontrollably by himself, and Ruthie was watching him intently while the teachers ignored him. It was hard to know why they ignored him, and it is possible that this was a child who cried regularly and often. Ruthie watched and then cradled herself inside the lap of one of her teachers; the teacher accepted her gently and gracefully while she herself seemed somewhat transfixed by the entire scene of the playground, staring out at it rather blankly.

The pack of boys was particularly remarkable to watch. Everywhere they went in the playground, someone ended up crying within minutes. One boy in particular was very good at pushing kids down when the teachers were not looking. It was an amazing scene, a three-ring circus of crying, combined with observers—adult and child—standing around in a state of quiet wonder, nobody very happy.

In my work in the public sphere, as I watch a situation closely for clues about the foundations of either conflict or harmony, I have to process a thousand different impressions. In the end, I always need to step back and ask myself, "What is going on here?" There is no way to see a situation clearly when you are buried beneath a thousand impressions. It is necessary to distill what you have seen before you start forming conclusions.

When I reflected on what I saw in the day-care center playground, what struck me first was what I didn't see: there was no abuse, no one losing their temper or flying into a rage. There was nothing being done by the adults that was wrong per se, but something was missing, which allowed pandemonium to rule.

These were just initial impressions; it took me a long time and a great deal of patience to form conclusions. I remember watching and listening to many conversations in the halls among parents, administrators and teachers, parents and children, and the children themselves. I have adopted the habit of examining what people put on their walls, and this is particularly important in schools. What schools display on their walls visually represents the educational messages that the adults want the kids to internalize. To some degree it also represents what administrators and teachers want the parents to see, because a school is also a place of buying and selling: parents are buying education, and administrators and teachers are selling it, making it attractive for the consumer. What they choose to highlight on the walls—and what is absent—can be very revealing.

Most schools have posters that emphasize things to be learned, such as basic math or reading skills, and they also sometimes have values-oriented posters. I remember, for example, seeing one poster in another school that said, Attitude Is Everything, with two kids giving each other a high-five. In this day-care center virtually all the posters were of an intellectual sort, emphasizing things to be learned. That combined with the atmosphere in the playground taught me much about my daughter and her schoolmates.

I also have become amazed at how much you can learn about any given institution, company, or family by watching intently the day-to-day behavior of its principal leaders. One day-care center, the first one Ruthie ever went to, was led by an amazing young woman. I was astonished at how young the administrator was, in her twenties I believe. She did not look or dress any older than the students I was teaching in university, but what a strong, quiet presence she had in that school! I walked down the hall with her and I felt that I was in the presence of someone who was in complete control. She knew every child by name; she popped her head into this place and that place, tidying up here and there. She had a quiet but commanding and loving presence that set the tone for a school that was in her control. At the other day-care center I don't ever remember seeing the administrator in the hallways. The hallways were crowded with kids' backpacks, everyone struggling to get by. Something was missing.

What I sensed was missing was an ethos. What I mean by *ethos* is a certain kind of spirit to a place, a guiding way of being that gives everyone direction, a role, a set of moral or social values that are enthusiastically embraced as defining the nature of the community. What I concluded from watching silently, from a distance, the day-care center that Ruthie reacted against, was that the center was too much an administrative entity. There was not enough of an ethical foundation of meaning to the place. This does not mean that the administrator was not a good person or perfectly professional, but she had not found a way to move beyond an administrative role to a leadership role, and it reflected itself in the smallest cues from the environment.

This emptiness emanating from the top left the teachers without a foundation to create, maintain, and defend a truly happy community of children. Conflicts and bullying, instead of being periodic interruptions that could be dealt with proactively, became an overarching and defining reality that left everyone just alright most of the time but never really flourishing and joyous. The kids just did not shriek with joy enough in this center, not as much as I had seen in several other successful centers.

An important caution is in order at this point. If my brief observations were to lead to absolute conclusions about the day-care center, without those conclusions being combined with other knowledge that I had, my reaction would have been interesting but premature. Seeing is a critical part of knowing what is wrong and what needs to be done, but if done without the other healing steps, such observation can lead to unfair conclusions. The power of observation should be combined especially with the previous step of hearing. It is the combination that strengthens our conclusions about what is wrong in a bad situation, and what needs to be made right.

Watching for Good Leadership

Leadership is such a powerful thing that one can often tell the personality of a leader from the atmosphere of the place he or she holds sway. If a day-care center, a community center, or a place of business is welcoming but somewhat disorganized, it is likely that the leader is like that. If it is efficient but lacking heart, it is likely that the leader is suppressing or not sharing herself with the community that she has created.

Due to several moves, Ruthie and my other daughter, Lexi, were in a number of day-care centers and schools when they were little. The excellent atmospheres in other centers were felt almost the moment I stepped in the door. The most important thing I noticed was the level of sheer joy the adults expressed to see each child. Walking down the hallway was an event for every child in which he or she would be greeted numerous times enthusiastically. I sensed a value system at work that set the tone for all the interactions.

In Ruthie's class at her first day-care center, there was a girl who was hitting others often, and I sensed that she had problems at home but it was unclear exactly what they were. There was also a teacher who seemed to us to be a bit rough on the kids, yelling rather often. No school is perfect, and no set of kids comes without challenges, but the amazing thing is that these problems did not overwhelm the school atmosphere. The ethic of the school, its feel, was intact, and the leadership of the school made sure of that.

The Healthy and the Destructive in Community

Seeing is a vital tool of engagement within communities of all kinds, not just children's day-care centers. Whether you engage successfully in these situations or accidentally plunge yourself into conflict may depend on your powers of observation. I remember an incident in a synagogue that I visited on a trip. I watched in amazement during one Saturday afternoon meal of celebration, as one man took a bottle of soda and, seemingly without warning, sprayed another man with the soda! He was clearly in a rage, his face was beet red even before the incident, and, from the moment I saw him, I sensed that he was a man in almost a perpetual state of indignation. He rarely smiled, and his children seemed rigid and in fear of him.

Curiously, this incident did not lead to a fistfight or retaliation. In fact, just a few moments later these two men were praying at the evening service in the same room, along with the rest of the community, joining together for the necessary quorum to constitute a praying community. There were no apologies, but the appointed time for prayer came and everything went on as usual.

I watched all of this and I asked myself, "What is going on here?" On the one hand, how could this disagreement have so few outlets through words that it resulted in this public act of physical humiliation, and on the other hand, how did this incident not lead to a spiral of violence? In fact it seems to have been suspended or broken up by evening prayers. How did prayer time stop this incident in its tracks? There were many unanswered questions.

There were aspects of this incident that I could see and

learn from on that day, while many other things remained a mystery. I saw that the one who sprayed the soda, Gary, was a troubled man, either perpetually angry at life, or at his standing in this community, or both. Evidence from the relationship to his children suggested that the problems went deep. I also later learned that Gary had had some serious and unresolved business disputes with others in the community, including the man he sprayed, who seemed particularly prone to speak up about these matters. It turned out that the comment that led to the spraying incident was a cynical aside about Gary's financial failures and what he owed everyone.

As much as I realized that this culture was at a disadvantage when it came to honest verbal communication or skills of reconciliation, I also saw that it was at a distinct advantage in terms of established social/religious norms. We usually think of rigid rituals as creating intolerance and a lack of good human relations, but this is not always true. There is a positive side to community rituals that goes unrecognized. As we noted earlier on, one of the biggest dangers of conflict is the way in which participants become addicted, as it were, to a drama. It is a ritual dance of enemies in which everyone feels compelled to ratchet up conflict to more and more intense levels until there is some act of decisive violence. This act in turn creates the cycle anew with an added spirit of revenge.

In this instance, the rituals and times of prayer not only prevented the second man from indulging in what we call the action-reaction spiral of conflict, it even led to the two of them praying together a few minutes later! Effectively, the rituals of normal religious life preempted the rituals of violence. Put another way, the drama of violence was replaced by the drama of community prayer in which these men needed each other.

Praying together by no means solved the conflict, and I suspect that the conflict remains unresolved to this day. But on that Saturday, the community's normal moral and spiritual functions did impose a measure of civility that prevented an escalation of violence, and that is not a small matter in human relations. The pressure of community conformity, of tradition, and of ritual is sometimes an antidote to the ritual of conflict.

I learned that evening that even when we are furious with each other, if we are part of one community, or one household, we should value the rituals that bring us together, whether those be songs, prayers, games, sports, board meetings, or meals. Such rituals are especially important when we are angry at each other. They do not solve the problems, but they help remind us of our basic values as a community or a family. Of course, if leaders or parents force common rituals down people's throats, then that coercive act on its own can create destructive feelings. The key is to subtly generate broad communal attachment to these rituals, even in the face of adversity, or especially in the face of adversity. We will discuss this more in the next to last step, Do.

Seeing Beyond First Impressions

Making an effort to see a situation from a removed perspective is an especially important tool in dispelling first impressions that can lead to conflict and animosity. For example, one of the social science experts I met through a public-speaking engagement, Dr. Robinson, had trouble getting along with his peers. Whenever he was involved in an intellectual exchange, everything had to go his way, and every theory had to relate back to his own.

I remember one episode in which I was quite taken with a speech that Dr. Robinson and I attended. I thought the keynote speaker, Dr. Wachovski, was particularly brilliant and had made many good points, although his theories were clearly different from Dr. Robinson's. Robinson reacted with hostility toward Wachovski, and I was troubled by this reaction, especially because I felt that he had embarrassed Wachovski in public by not showing him sufficient respect. I reacted angrily to his behavior because public dishonor hits a nerve in me, and I also happened to agree more with Wachovski's ideas.

I decided to probe matters further, and each time we met I engaged Robinson in some probing conversations in order to learn more, but it turned out that I turned too quickly to conversation and did not step back enough to *observe*. For example, I mentioned in passing some ideas similar to those of Wachovski, and Robinson got a suspicious look on his face. He clearly began to distance himself from me. I could not understand how a man of this level of accomplishment could be so easily threatened by the slightest deviation from his ideas, especially at this late stage of his life.

It occurred to me that I should step back from engaging direct conversation with Robinson for a time and revert to simply watching. Sometimes we simply talk too much, and in so doing we miss the opportunity to observe, and so I watched Robinson's reactions in several meetings, listening carefully to his words and his critiques of other speakers as well as the leading questions he was asking. I practiced a combination of listening and watching. I played the encounters over in my mind time and time again, long after the meetings ended. With results in hand from hearing and seeing—these two steps complement each other particularly well—I started to realize things about Robinson that I had never understood before.

Wachovski is healthier and younger than Robinson, although he is also approaching retirement age. Robinson is affiliated with a more prestigious institution and is a good deal wealthier, but none of the wealth can give him back his youth or the world fame he once had. He had recently barely recovered from a life-threatening illness, and I discovered to my amazement that despite his prestige, a significant journal had refused to publish an article of his and instead chose to run an article by a colleague of Wachovski's. Things started to add up.

I surmised that Dr. Robinson was questioning whether

his life had been worthwhile. To him, every statement at odds with his intellectual positions represented an attack on the value of his life's work. He could not articulate this self-doubt, however. Rather it was something that I needed to see in order to create better relations and avoid predictable land mines in future encounters with Robinson. He is the one who really needed to go through a process of self-examination, but at least by going through the steps myself I could minimize conflict with him.

To create better relations with Robinson, my younger colleagues and I went out of our way on future occasions to honor this man's life, his contribution, to listen to him without debate, and to take him seriously. We paid him inordinate respect, more than should normally be necessary. Only after doing this would we be able to dispassionately discuss his ideas and have a professional relationship with Robinson.

In more recent interactions I have deliberately focused on honoring this man, particularly through questions and active listening, and even adjusting my body language to show respect. It has worked amazingly well, and our relationship has continued to improve. So often as we engage successful people, all we see is their success whereas all they are conscious of are their failures. This step reminds us to observe everything about a person so that when we do engage in conversation our interactions can succeed at a profound level.

Stepping Back to Watch
the Drama of Encounters

The more tense and dramatic a conflict is, the more important become your powers of observation. Seeing is essential
to surviving in a situation involving destructive conflict. In
the course of our travels, my colleague Ryan and I have continued to make relationships in a wide variety of venues. One
of the most unusual has been a set of relationships with religious clerics on both sides of the Israeli-Palestinian conflict
who have cultivated relationships themselves with political
and military leaders on both sides. The purpose of these exchanges has been to utilize cultural and religious resources for
peacemaking, especially because the political leaderships have
failed so badly to find a formula for coexistence and other
governments have utterly failed to be successful mediators.

Religious people in many conflicts around the world
have sometimes managed to create bridges between enemies
where nothing else seemed to work. Ryan and I, together
with many other friends, are committed on a more basic spiritual level to creating friendships in war, no matter what the
consequences or the usefulness of those friendships may be
in the final analysis. At the same time, it has been our hope
to create relationships with people who we think could be at
the forefront of more peaceful relationships with others, particularly if they are founded on sound moral principles of
human interaction.

One of the most memorable of these relationships was
with a Muslim Palestinian officer. Colonel Ibrahim is an ex-

traordinary person who, while not as powerful as some other political and military leaders, is highly placed and has a reputation for honesty and decency. I had heard about this man for some time and I was eager to meet him.

Meetings in this environment are always complicated and unpredictable. The religious clerics arranged to meet in a hotel in Jerusalem, and the topic of the meeting was to explore religious and cultural approaches to reconciliation between the two peoples, something the Colonel has supported for a long time. The meeting took place before the outbreak of hostilities in 2000, but even then relations were not terribly good. I walked into the lobby of the hotel, started asking questions of the clerics about the arrangements, and immediately got a little nervous.

There were no rooms reserved, and the only place to meet was in the lobby. There were a series of large lounge chairs in disparate locations and a great deal of open space. Not a great environment for privacy. We had a major Palestinian military leader coming with his entourage to a civilian Israeli hotel in broad daylight and several clerics in distinctive garb. The reason for this meeting was to meet with Ryan and me as American visitors. We decided to pull together some of the chairs and make a large circle off to the side of the lobby. The word *spectacle* comes to mind. Even before the Colonel arrived, I was not happy, and when he arrived I immediately watched his reaction. He was visibly uncomfortable, but we sat down anyway.

The Colonel is a distinguished Middle Eastern man,

and I was immediately impressed by his smiling eyes. His translator was extremely sharp and watched everything around him. They were not wearing their uniforms, I imagine by agreement with Israel. We began the meeting, and it was going well, but it became clear that more and more people in the hotel were noticing us, and some of the passersby were not happy. After about forty-five minutes it became clear that there were several plainclothes Israeli agents around us with earphones. The Colonel became plainly uncomfortable, and he politely ended the meeting.

Ryan and I reflected for hours on what we had seen as we went over every detail in our minds. It is so easy in such encounters to get lost in the dialogue itself, to focus on the words and ideas being exchanged but to forget what you see. Overly educated people are especially prone to miss such details. We concluded from what we saw, not from what was said, that the Colonel's honor had been compromised, perhaps even his security. *He* was the one who came to Jerusalem to see us, and yet he was made to feel vulnerable and suspect in an atmosphere in which dishonor is such a central part of the enemy relations. There was no private room, no tea, no meal, only a vulnerable atmosphere. Of course, no one intended for this to happen. The situation resulted from insufficient planning, poor resources, lack of coordination, and lack of foresight. But we should have imagined in advance such a delicate scenario and planned accordingly. We should have seen in advance what it would look like. Even though I was not in charge of the location choice, I felt foolish, like a novice at conflict work. The last thing we had intended was dishonor, but that is precisely what happened. We realized that honor and dignity are a rare experience and an even rarer consideration.

Ryan and I decided that we needed to show the Colonel by our further actions that we were determined to honor him in the way that he deserved. He had invited us to his headquarters in Palestine, Gaza City, several times, but we were reluctant to go due to timing issues—it would cut short our trip with many other people—and security considerations. We decided it was worth the loss of other meetings, and worth the risk, because this man was so different than and superior to the politicians and military men who had brought on so much of the violence from both sides. We needed to pursue this relationship at all costs.

I could not let that scene in the hotel lobby be our last encounter. It was amazing how closely aligned Ryan's intuitions and mine were on that day in the hotel lobby. We saw exactly the same things, the good aspects and the bad aspects. Seeing from a removed perspective can form an incredible bond between you and others as you seek to heal conflicts. Seeing is an exercise, a discipline, and a puzzle to be deciphered. Naturally you and your colleagues will sometimes observe different things, but the common exploration definitely creates a bond.

With some difficulty we went to Gaza a couple of days later. When we reached the Colonel's headquarters, he and his assistant greeted us with an overwhelming amount of appreciation. They treated us to a sumptuous meal of vege-tarian (Kosher) salads and Middle Eastern dishes. The Colonel sat with us and watched us eat, even though he was fasting that day for religious reasons. That in itself suggested an extraordinary level of hospitality and honor. There was not a single place in all of Israel and Palestine, before or since, in which I was treated with so much respect, and this was in the center of Palestinian military headquarters! So strange.

War is a devastating human experience affecting the lives of millions of people, but it contains within it the most bizarre contradictions. I've learned to live with those contra-dictions and tried to avoid losing my openness to extraordi-nary individuals and their goodness, but I couldn't do this without the power of seeing. To see requires that you look at every situation anew, to judge by what you see in front of you and suspend for a time all of your previous assumptions. This practice is indispensable in identifying turning points in con-flicts. Seeing in this way gives you an openness to people and to situations that could never exist if you stayed inside what you *think* you know about others.

It was really only after that trip to Gaza that Ryan and I realized how right we were in our observations of the Jerusalem meeting. The Colonel never said a negative word about the circumstances of the meeting, even when we probed the matter with him in Gaza, although he did offer a vague smile. Had we not engaged the skill of seeing we never would have understood what we needed to fix in this rela-tionship. Seeing is designed to prevent catastrophes of conflict and to help heal hurts that have already occurred. The relationship that we created then persists to this day and has become crucial to our work.

Opening Our Eyes to Enemies

Lessons learned from these experiences include the need to open our eyes and dispassionately view our adversaries. So much of the destructive aspect of human conflict comes from how blindly we walk through life, unaware of our impact on others at any given moment or what others are experiencing around us while we are absorbed in our own worlds. Our eyes are usually shut to the experiences of others, unless we train ourselves otherwise. This requires concentration on chains of events, how one event or one encounter leads to a series of others.

Practice in this art of observation teaches us how to trace conflict back to its most early stages and most subtle injuries. It is by detecting the earliest phases of hurtful behavior that we learn what needs to be reversed or prevented from happening in the first place. That is why a dispassionate memory is such an important aid in seeing. What I mean by *dispassionate* is that people often return to memories in order to reinforce their injuries, their prejudices, their anger. "Did you see the way that guy manipulated me? All that free advice he gave me? Not for my own good but in order to manipulate me. I am going to trace back in my mind every time I ever encountered him so I can prove that it was all about manipulation." In this way memory becomes a mere support system for conflict. But dispassionate memory of encounters can serve quite a different function if we have taken the earlier steps of healing as a prelude to seeing.

If we are truly prepared to see then we will remember details of our encounters and reconstruct what went wrong between us and others. We will practice remembering all encounters, but especially those in which we played a major role. This takes time and patience and a willingness to go over details again and again, but the benefits will be substantial. When you start to remember exactly when someone you are in conflict with said or did the first thing that hurt you, when the first time was that someone starting acting strangely toward you as if you had done something wrong, you may be well on your way to understanding the real dynamics of the conflict.

It is equally important to trace back in your memory the details of your good encounters, when, for instance, you felt really good or when others showed you great kindness. Here you may discover opportunities to restore good relations. A focused observation of the positive will give you the power to engender more of those positive encounters in your life.

The Unseen Can Lead to the Extraordinary

Sometimes adversaries are relatively clear about what they want, but we need always to concentrate and see if other, unspoken needs are behind their rancor and dissatisfaction. At other times our adversaries will propose solutions that are not acceptable to us, and in fact an examination of their "solution" will reveal other, unspoken desires and needs. To summarize lessons learned from our exploration, it behooves us in such complicated circumstances to always pay attention to two things: one, what to watch for, and two, what to do.

What to watch for: Examine the visceral reactions that people have to each other, and to you. Are they averting their eyes from you, are they holding their breath when they speak to you? Is someone warm at first and then cold and callous without explanation? What happened in between? Who comes up to you when you enter a room full of people, and who avoids you? Are they really avoiding you or are they distracted? How can you tell the difference? Let us say that you have set the stage for a meeting between you and your adversary. How is he reacting to the surroundings? Why? How much can you learn just by these observations? Can you train yourself to be better attuned to the art of observation even when surrounded by friends, not adversaries, so that you notice subtle hints of trouble that might crop up when you meet new people? Such observation takes discipline and practice, but it often leads to more successful encounters and relationships, especially if it is followed upon by the rest of the Eight Steps.

What to do: All of the Eight Steps are leading you toward knowing what to actively do to make your life better, to prevent bad relations, and to heal those relationships that have been damaged. Dr. Ries Vanderpol, a psychologist and survivor of the Holocaust, writes a great deal about resilience as the key characteristic of people who are able to survive in the worst of circumstances and even thrive. Some people have an incredible ability to use their powers of observation to assess situations and to thrive in their relationships no matter how bad their childhood experiences or circumstances may have been.

I believe deeply that such people use their senses adeptly, which is one of the reasons that I have focused the healing steps on the human senses. Above all, the resilient person is always heading toward decisive action. Decisive action requires decisive listening and decisive seeing. It requires a retooling of the senses toward what they can teach us about the best forms of interactions with others. There are those who watch the world in despair, and those who watch in order to learn and do. This does not mean that the poet's eye for the tragic in the human condition is misdirected, or that we should avert our eyes from misery in the world. It just means that if we are to be happy, if we are to be resilient as individuals and as members of communities, then we should aspire to using our natural senses, such as seeing and hearing, to their fullest capacity in order to heal conflicts whenever and wherever we can.

STEP SIX: IMAGINE

Visions of the Future

Imagination is something that we rarely think of as a way to heal and become happy as human beings. We separate flights of fantasy into some less serious part of the human experience, like fairy tales or entertainment. But imagination is responsible for much of human happiness—as well as for human misery when it is used badly.

It is never too late to heal old conflicts with the power of imagination. After examining ourselves and others as described

IMAGINE: TO STEP BACK FROM THE WEB OF CONFLICT AND ENVISION WAYS THAT WILL UTTERLY TRANSFORM OUR LIVES AND RELATIONSHIPS.

in the first three steps, and after carefully observing our environment closely per the next two, our imagination is freed to find solutions that before would have seemed unacceptable. For example, one of the oldest and most damaging conflicts in our nation's history involves the evils of slavery. There is so much more to be done to heal the wounds of that terrible period and the wars and injustice that it created in its wake, but healing is possible and indeed has begun, in seemingly little ways that can make a big difference.

Imaginative Healing

Colonial Williamsburg, Virginia, provides a wonderful tableau of life during colonial times, as workers dress up in period costumes and reenact the customs and day-to-day activities of our early settlers. This popular tourist spot is a treasured destination for thousands of Americans every year, but in 1999 a somewhat controversial decision was made to reenact the slave sales that actually took place there. At first some groups opposed this program as abusive toward African-Americans, but soon it became apparent that the scenes of the slave sales were cathartic and healing for many people, both black and white. People yelled at the actors playing slave traders and owners and rallied behind the abolitionists. It was as if people had the chance to go back and challenge the evils of the time, and they embraced the opportunity.

I myself participated in a march in Richmond that recreated the route that slaves were forced to take, a march that included a visit to the appalling living quarters so many were forced to endure. During the march, which was sponsored by Initiatives of Change, an international movement active in more than fifty countries, we walked together, Americans and visitors from abroad, black and white, Jew and Christian, northerners and southerners, and many local residents from in and around Richmond. We entered the slave stables and faced the shackles—an incredibly painful and moving moment. To visit these places as a white person is one experience, and to visit as a black person is another experience, but to visit as a group of both blacks and whites together is particularly powerful.

In my reconciliation work around the world, I have seen that when descendents of victims visit a place of suffering with others, often the bad memories are re-imagined and re-experienced in a transformative way. In this case, African-Americans may come to feel that their isolation and pain finally have been shared and acknowledged, that their hurt is now public knowledge and they no longer need to be burdened by feelings of alienation, shame, or anxiety. White visitors, at the same time, may feel a weight lifted from their conscience, as sharing the experience with others can lessen the guilt that they may have hidden, even from themselves.

The healing power of groups, when they respectfully imagine the past and reinvent their present relations, almost automatically leads individuals to envision a different future. The imagination it took to plan the Enslaving Virginia program at Williamsburg and the slavery walk in Richmond, and to anticipate their impact, was truly extraordinary. It is an example of working with our dreams and fantasies, even our terrible fantasies of the past, but all in order to create positive and healing changes in relationships, in the present and for the future.

For the step of Imagine, we should ask ourselves, each

in the context of our own lives, what our deepest hopes are, what conflicts we want most to solve, how we could imagine changing these situations with the help of others, even with our adversaries. What dare we dream? Who must we dream with in order for the dreams to begin to create reality?

Returning to the slave march for a moment, I remember, as if it were yesterday, an unbelievable scene. At the end of the march, thousands of flowers were released on the water near the docks where the slaves arrived in Richmond. High above the bank of the James River, hundreds of us, black and white, stood in silence watching the flowers float away. Truly, it was as if we were burying people at sea. Through our imaginations we went back in time and grieved for the dead who never survived the voyage from Africa and for the broken lives of those who passed through this port to a harsh reality that was not of their making, to a life that was not a real life.

This profound experience set the stage for us as a group to move toward the final step in healing, Speak. I remember witnessing a very old, bent-over white southern woman rise before the gathered group, go to the microphone, and, in an almost inaudible whisper, begin to tell the tale of how she had been raised as a child. After uttering the word "plantation," her voice broke and she began to weep. Most of us just sat there in astonishment, but a middle-aged black woman stood up, walked up to the microphone, and embraced the elderly white woman. No one who was there that day will forget what either woman did.

Sometimes it is difficult to imagine how much one such moment can link so dramatically our collective hopes, our memories, our very perception of reality. I can no longer conceive of slavery in the American South without envisioning those two women embracing, the young black woman comforting the older white woman. What a reversal of history, what nobility of character in these two brave women, both children of the South. How strange and awesome is the unfolding of human history.

This moment illustrates the power of the courageous use of imagination in healing and reconciliation. These healing interpersonal exchanges would not have taken place if the organizers had not imagined the slave march, and we would not have the image of those two brave women seared into our memories if either woman had not found the courage to imagine themselves before that microphone.

Rob Corcoran was one of the organizers of this extraordinary event, but he credits Ben Campbell of Richmond for coming up with the vision of black and white walking together the path of the slaves. The flower ritual began in the imagination of yet another person, Margaret Palmer. One act of bold imagination cascaded into many acts of imagination, all designed to bring healing and reconciliation to the heart of Richmond. Rob told me, "The walk broke the silence, and seemed to release the heavy weight of history. It left us free to talk, to begin a conversation." Through the hard work of many, the dream became a reality.

Without the power of imagination, there can be no

solution to the greatest conflicts, no real improvement in the quality of our lives. Imagination, when used carefully and constructively, can solve our problems. The key is to free ourselves of preconceived ideas about our adversaries and about ourselves so we are able to conceive of new ways of living together outside destructive conflict.

How Not to Use Imagination

As with other kinds of human potential, imagination can be used destructively or constructively. We cannot heal the wounds of conflict without first recognizing this paradox. Imagination may be healthy or merely harmless when it involves inventing alternate worlds and realities as a way to take our minds off the stresses of daily life or as a creative way to examine life from a different vantage point. Even for children it can be beneficial to imagine who they want to be in the future. It is healthy for children to imagine themselves during play as teachers, students, doctors, veterinarians, and other professional roles. My four year old announced one day that she will be a dog keeper when she grows up. "Great!" I said.

Imagination can cause trouble, however, when we have dreams that require other people to be or behave in a certain way. We may imagine that everyone in our family should be exactly who we want and need them to be. The same goes for the place where we work, and even the city and country in which we live. Political ambition has led to visions that perhaps seemed sublime on paper but that have ended up endlessly bloody because the vision was not shared, or was not created in a way that would combine many different visions of a shared future. Many religious visions, for example, seem quite beautiful, but when combined with political and military control they become tragic nightmares rather than spiritual dreams.

Such morally irresponsible visions inevitably lead to human injury. That is not to say that we human beings do not have a right or even a responsibility to imagine better political worlds than the ones we reside in. In this respect, imagination is a core part of human freedom. But we have to recognize the real misery that can result if the imagined worlds do not include a way for each person to participate equally, or to stand apart from that dream and create their own.

For example, communism is partly based on the dream of sharing property equally, of escaping the injustices of a world in which there are always the rich and the poor. But the cure turned out to be worse than the disease in the hands of extremists in Russia who brutalized millions of people for decades, justified endless murder and theft, all in the name of equality. In the Middle Ages a beautiful religious idea of an eternal soul turned into a nightmare as brutal extremists justified the torture of thousands of people whose religious beliefs were deemed heretical, all in the name of purifying their eternal souls by torturing their bodies. Equality for all is a beautiful dream, and an eternal soul is a beautiful idea, but they turn into nightmares when combined with intolerant constructs of the world and the abandonment of ethical limits on our behavior.

Another way that imagination can cause trouble is when we get stuck in fear. We are afraid of our opponents and what they could do to us, and we imagine the worst things that may happen if we do not defend ourselves. We may then get into a war mode, wherein every step we take must be geared toward defending ourselves against future attack. Some of this fear may be legitimate, based on real evidence of past actions, but some of it is based on an unreasonable exercise of our imagination. There is no question, for example, that the United States faces a dangerous enemy today who is willing and eager to kill civilians, but September 11 did nothing to help us distinguish between constructive and destructive uses of our imagination. Our worst nightmares were confirmed, and yet greater nightmares loom. But watching the constant coverage of the war on terrorism on television can lead us to be fooled into imagining the worst all the time. It takes great care in such situations not to let the darkest part of our imagination overwhelm our other abilities, such as the capacity for self-examination or the ability to see, listen, and learn from the world around us.

There are other ways that imagination can cause conflict. People place a lot of hope in their dreams, and if those dreams don't come true they can grow frustrated or bitter. We can see this in observing children. I never cease to be amazed at the dynamics of hope and disappointment in my children. If we don't mention the zoo as a place to go on a particular day, they won't suggest it on their own. But if we mention it, plan for it, and then can't go for some reason, no matter how legitimate the reason, well, there is hell to pay! It is as if their lives will come to an end. We adults learn to suppress the lion's share of our emotions, but the way children act clue us in to what is really going on in *our* inner lives. Children hate frustrated dreams with a passion, and their wild disappointment seems to match or exceed their wild burst of joy when you first planted the vision of them at the zoo inside their lovely heads. That is exactly what goes on inside many adults, except they keep it suppressed until it bursts out in some way that is often as surprising to them as it is to others.

When people develop hope, which is a sign of a good imagination, their devastation when things do not come true makes it hard to move forward with healing. This is one of the great dangers of trying to heal other people's conflicts, because giving hope is critical to a political process of peacemaking, but when that hope continuously goes unfulfilled, then the dream becomes a torturous tease that makes people even angrier than they were before.

That is why politicians should focus on what they *can* do in conflicts, what they *can* deliver by way of progress toward solutions, but they should not manipulate the dreams of their constituents for political ends.

It is the same at home and at work. Exercises in positive imagination should never be used as a way to divert attention from real needs that people need fulfilled now, and it is important to be aware of when our dreams are being manipulated for political advantage. If, for example, my daughter is upset because I am considering not continuing her ice skating lessons due to an injury she sustained, the last thing I should do is divert her attention by "buying her off" with talk of a vacation we can go on. Rather, I should deal in the moment with her anger and also examine honestly whether I am giving in to my own fears about her safety. Politically it is advantageous for me to win the family argument and to manage her feelings by cleverly introducing great imaginative scenarios, but it is manipulative, dishonest to my daughter, disrespectful of her intelligence, and dishonest to myself. This is misplaced imagination.

When our disappointment with unrealized dreams becomes overwhelming, there is a powerful human tendency to blame other people for our problems. It's a psychological defense mechanism. Even if other people are partially responsible for hurting our chances of reaching our dreams, the problem is that attachment to dreams and fantasy can be so overwhelming emotionally that it prevents reasoned reflection and a sense of balance in evaluating who or what is to blame for our failed dreams, especially if that person is us.

Getting caught up in blaming others not only leads to paranoia, scapegoating, and unnecessary conflicts, but it also gives great power to our adversaries. For example, returning to our response to 9/11, what is slowly dawning on Americans is the painful reality that millions of people around the world hate us just for being Americans. This reality strikes at the very core of the American dream, part of which is to be a nation admired, a shining beacon of democracy, freedom, and prosperity. But we cannot afford to lash out indiscriminately, to scapegoat whole groups of people, to insult the prophets of other people's religions. This kind of paranoia and destructive hatred is precisely the enemy we are fighting that has infected cultures overseas. It also feeds the cause of those who want to bring out the worst in us to justify their violence. We can do better than this, especially in a free society, by adjusting our imaginations to the lessons learned from the other steps of healing conflict, particularly the gift of honest self-examination, at a personal and a political level.

Finally, another way that our imagination hurts us is when it actually kills our hopes. Sometimes mourning over lost dreams is so wrenching that cynical visions prevent any legitimate place inside some people for alternative or new dreams. An obsession with some dreams can lead to others being stillborn. A father's dreams of becoming wealthy can become so obsessive that he lets die his wife and child's more simple dreams of taking two hours every Sunday to enjoy the outdoors as a family, together.

Loss of dreams can cause conflicts because there is no hope for creative alternatives to present difficulties, and so, in despair, we throw up our hands and surrender ourselves to fighting and endless struggle. The father may throw himself more deeply into arguments with his partner over money rather than re-tool his imagination to see the beautiful and attainable reality that his family members see, but that he has not imagined.

This makes the step of Imagine that much more important. When conflicts or tragedies go on for a long time, it usually means that we must address the past as well as build, together with others, a shared imagined future. Mourning and letting go of old dreams is sometimes a key part of building new and better ones.

Craig and the Company

I met Craig in Colorado at a convention dealing with development and poverty issues. He has worked for the same company for more than twenty years. He was at the height of his intellectual strength and accomplishment when, instead of pursuing an academic path that would have brought him great prestige, he chose to work for a company. The company Craig joined marketed a product that promised to not only turn a great profit but also transform the world in terms of the availability of food. Craig had a strong working-class background with a penchant for social justice, and it meant a great deal to him to produce something good for the world. But he often fantasized about what his life would have been like had he pursued the career in reasearch that could have followed from his degree in nutrition.

Craig had always had a difficult relationship with his family, who were undereducated. This left him feeling extraordinarily insecure about himself despite a truly impressive intellect.

Craig's major problem was that he allowed the company's flaws to become his. In his lack of confidence he had completely overidentified with this company's goals and practices. As he began to separate himself mentally from the fate of the company, he began to enter into a crisis.

Curious conflicts arose. He started developing a nasty tendency to point out how stupid his colleagues were. Certainly it is true that they could not match him intellectually, but Craig seemed to obsess about this inequality in ways that alienated coworkers and superiors alike. He became depressed and irritable, alternately defending the company with unnatural anger when it was attacked by others and excoriating its failings on his own. Leaving the company at his age was almost impossible, and he was not prepared for separation anyway. He needed the good money he was making to pay a substantial mortgage, but he was trapped in an identity crisis that was provoking conflicts with many people.

Craig started reading voraciously, as if he were looking for answers to the meaning of his life. Indeed, Craig's professional crisis seemed to be provoking a religious crisis for him as well.

In terms of the specific relationships that were bringing conflict into Craig's life, there is no question that he needed to engage the Eight Steps of healing that we have outlined. All of his relationships could have benefited. My sense was that Craig needed to focus especially on Imagine. Traps and prisons that we find ourselves in, especially ones that have been built over decades, take as their first hostage our power of imagination. We are trapped in past choices and mistakes, and we cannot see any way out. We do engage in fantasies, but not healthy ones, and we fantasize excessively about the past, about what might have been. In this way, regret comes to tyrannize the psyche.

It is not altogether bad to indulge our worst fears from time to time. Such cathartic honesty can be an important stage in healing. Fantasizing about past choices can be healthy if we use those fantasies to figure out what we really want out of our lives in the present and in the future. But it is destructive if we do this constantly with no plan for over-coming those feelings.

I had listened to Craig's anger so many times that at some point I was not really listening anymore. One day, I'm not certain why, I really heard him, and I realized that he was crying out for respect, for respect of his mind and his intelligence, and that the lack of respect from others, and especially his lack of self-respect, had been his greatest loss in life. But I also was keenly aware that counseling him to leave his job at his age, without transferable skills, was perilous and pre-sumptuous on my part.

I encouraged Craig to write. Much of what he wrote was directed at criticizing the company's practices. This was not what I was looking for, but it was not altogether bad. Writing is healthy for most people, especially those who feel frustrated. As Craig and I talked more and more about his writing projects, one day it dawned on me that he and I might explore together some issues in nutrition and its rela-tionship to the peacemaking capacity of human beings. Craig was delighted. Someone who he respected was no longer looking at him as a businessman but was respecting him as a thinker. It's the kind of respect that he craved.

As Craig and I fantasized together about the project, we were also unintentionally fantasizing about Craig's future identity, about how he could continue to work in the company while at the same time engaging in writing and research on his own time that would transform his sense of self, especially if, through collaboration, he managed to get published. Craig envisioned himself lecturing from time to time to audiences about his research because his most important goal was to stimulate his imagination. This is what brought him self-respect and meaning, this is what he longed for, and the process of imagining a research career began to transform his sense of self. Craig was more at peace with himself, and as a result his relationships began to heal. He no longer needed to build his future on the ruins of others' because now he was free to create new worlds in and through his new sense of identity. We never did do the project together, but it did not matter because it seemed to spur a burst of creativity on his part.

Forget about How to Get from Here to There

Craig and I deliberately let go of trying to figure out his problems in the company in favor of indulging his fantasies of a different life. That may appear impractical to some readers, but in fact it is essential. The most important step in using imagination wisely is imagining yourself in a completely different set of relationships and circumstances. The key is to let go of working on, at least for the moment, how to get from here to there, from the conflict we find ourselves in to the ideal solution. The point is to just indulge new scenarios, to build them in our minds or on paper and to think about how they would look and feel. It is even better if this can be done together with others, and best if you find you are able to do this together with those you are in conflict with.

The problem in so many human conflicts is that our very efforts to solve them actually trap us. Our minds try to figure out what is wrong by going over and over a seemingly endless array of details, but while we recite in our heads who said and did what to whom, our minds become a prison. Each time we focus on these details or plan our next step, we get more and more caught inside this prison of our own making. At the coffee shops where I write I often overhear conversations about conflicts, and what amazes me is the number of details that people have memorized about their conflicts. "He said . . . , then she said . . . , then I said . . ." The dialogues seem to go on forever, and yet there is no way out. There is no perception going on, no imagination, no stepping back from the web of details to a different future.

Courageous and free imagination is the way out of this prison. It is as if one part of us is designed to get us out of troubles that are caused by other parts! Courageous imagination is an act of resilience in the face of trouble, and it is something that some people have naturally but that everyone can train and cultivate.

Dreaming with Colonels, Rabbis, and Sheikhs

Escaping the web of conflict by freeing the imagination can seem absurd in the midst of war, but that is exactly where I learned the most about its value. I suppose one of the most memorable moments in my life occurred in 1999 inside a military compound in Ramallah, which is effectively the capital of the Palestinian territories. Here I found myself sitting with military and religious leaders from both sides of the Middle East conflict, yet the atmosphere was anything but warlike. It was the opposite—a place of great warmth and respect. These people had established relationships over many years, and what amazed me that afternoon was the way sufficient trust had been created between these people to freely share their imagined futures.

It takes a lot of trust to share a dream, but it cannot be the end of the odyssey. If all one does with adversaries is share dreams, then it is a cruel tease. Imagining must culminate in new relationships, a new way in which we speak and treat one another. What I witnessed that day in Ramallah was the combination of profound personal relations built on the principles of the Eight Steps. The courage to share dreams of a different Middle East, of a time when national boundaries will be less important, when religious practices will bring people together rather than tear them apart, was something that we were modeling in that gathering. We were also laying plans to bring that reality to an audience of millions, but unfortunately those dreams were never allowed to bear fruit. Violence overwhelmed the situation and made further meetings impossible.

It is true that there were people in that room and in that building who were using this gathering merely as political cover. But that was not true of the majority, and the relations that I hoped to facilitate, strengthen, and encourage could serve as an interim step toward peacemaking in the future. War is so injurious to so many millions of people that it takes an agonizingly large number of confidence-building steps over years between people of good will before hard-won relationships overwhelm the forces of hatred. It was amazing how long that dreaming session went on in Ramallah, but it was time well spent considering the relationships that emerged from those meetings.

Imagination in the right hands is an act of bold resilience. It is an assertion of the human right to dream, of the human right to change our circumstances when we so wish, no matter how slowly that change may come.

Living with Contradiction

Another way that imagination helps heal serious conflict is that it gives us the ability to live creatively with contradictory situations. We learn to build a vision of new possibilities, to see ourselves there inside those possibilities, and then also to see our adversaries there. On that day in Ramallah there were people in the room with religious and political visions that seemed impossible to reconcile. There were people in that room who had literally killed others. Certainly there are many religious people in the world, Muslim, Jewish, and Christian, who would not have understood or agreed with the imagined worlds we were building. We were planning for a Middle East in which holy places were both honored and shared, a place in which political boundaries would cease to matter, in the form of economic confederations of states. We were building a reality in which the content of character and the mode of treatment of each other was a far more precious religious possession than exclusive obsession over a piece of land or a specific location. There are millions of people around the world who would celebrate these developments, while others would find it difficult to imagine such an exchange in the context of so much death, destruction, and betrayal. But that is the very business of dreaming and imagination—a kind of preparation for healing when it will become possible, even when currently there appears to be no hope. History suggests that the most exalted dreams are born right in the middle of the most hopeless realities, but then time marches on and what appeared to be absurd dreaming turns out to be the basis for new realities.

Those Ramallah conversations were crucial building blocks for further work. Since that time several of the figures involved have continued to be among the only voices of sanity in an insane situation. They have marched forward in meeting after meeting, including more and more fellow travelers from across the world. Even in the midst of an impossible situation, we further solidified relationships on that day, which then set the stage for building more and more relationships that will lay the foundation of a new reality yet. In the process of peacemaking, such small victories are how history is made.

In my own life I have come to expect contradiction. I revel in paradox as if it is an old friend. Many people suffer from conflict because they deny, avoid, and evade its reality. They say everything is fine at work when clearly it is not. They have no instincts for living with contradictions such as, "I love the work I do, even though some of my colleagues make me crazy," or, "I feel incredibly close to Mom, and yet I know that sometime in the next week, like clockwork, she will insult me." People who cannot cope with such contradictions will live in denial and suffering, or, alternatively, they will demonize and destroy good relationships.

Life has taught me that you shouldn't accept either one of those options. Childhood memories of family, for example, are often mixed. Some of us remember conflicts and fights between our parents that seemed horrendous at the time, while others experienced family life that was in almost constant turmoil. And yet most of us can remember at least one special moment, however brief, that contradicts our negative view. It could involve something as basic as food. I remember fondly the cupcakes fresh from the bakery near our summer cottage, and I miss Saturday nights with my father's fried sausages. My parents catered my Bar Mitsvah celebration at the age of thirteen, and for years after we marveled at how the guests thought it was so delicious that they ate virtually everything, right down to the decorative parsley. We have a picture of my father proudly holding two giant pickle jars that he had personally filled, with rows more in the background, and there was never a Saturday celebration at my house where the extended family did not leave the table dazed by the array of food that my father had prepared. In spite of the family conflicts, those were good times.

Positive Imagination in Child Rearing

Living with contradiction, living with tension, and balancing our roles are also essential for child rearing, and imagination is critical to dealing with those daily struggles. Small children are needy and eager for our constant input. They want us and need us to be their helpers, teachers, comforters, boundary setters, entertainers, comedians, cooks, maids, secretaries, playmates—all at the same time that they insist on testing the boundaries of their independence! We ask them to balance dependence and independence as precariously as we try to balance caring for them and teaching them to live without our help.

We want our children to always defer to our judgment, but on the other hand we want them to brush their teeth on their own, get snacks for themselves, get their own pencil or markers, tie their shoes, and a whole host of other daily tasks. One child I know had a major challenge with being too dependent, while his sibling was just the opposite. The first instinct of parents may be to compare their children: "Why can't you get up in the morning like your sister and put your clothes on without us? Why is everything a struggle?" I remember thinking about this as I observed this pattern of behavior on the playground at my child's school, and I immediately thought to myself, "Vision it." I sat down with this overly dependent boy and gave him a lot of compliments about all the good things that I saw him doing (all true). Then I asked him, "Can you see yourself getting up in the morning, jumping out of bed before anyone comes in your room, jumping into your clothes, and jumping downstairs to get breakfast? Can you see your parents proud of you?" Something must have clicked, because the next day that is exactly what he did. After that, getting up became far less of a struggle. It was as if the cycle of struggle and dependency was embedded and habitual but really only lacking an imagined alternative scenario. No one wanted or enjoyed the struggle, but a new vision was necessary in order to tip the balance in favor of more creative actions and habits.

In order to cope with conflict, adults need to rethink simplistic dreams and aspire to dreams that embrace some degree of contradiction or tension. No one can truly live with others without this capacity. Few people I know have not experienced this tension in their religious lives, for example. Most people alive today experience some degree of tension between simple, traditional religious beliefs and traditions and contemporary ethical and social issues. No one could have predicted how overpopulated the planet would become, how much people from many religions would be freely mixing as equals in democratic societies, how equal men and women would become in their accomplishments and opportunities, how much science would revolutionize our understanding of the world and its realities from trillions of miles away right down to the world inside our DNA. Yet these realities challenge many assumptions of traditional religious faith and practice, and they have forced us to live with even more contradiction.

Some solve that contradiction by turning their backs on empirical realities or by turning their backs on religious tradition. Some refuse either option and live with the creative tension of religion and modern life. My family cannot surrender the timeless truths and wisdom of Judaism. We cannot, at the same time, refuse to acknowledge the timeless wisdom of other religious traditions, nor the foundations of secular democracy, philosophy, and science, all of which we believe emanate from the grandeur of God's positive intentions.

There is an ancient rabbinic story that says that God revealed himself to Moses, the Lawgiver and liberator of his people, through a symbol of peace. That symbol is the burning bush that Moses, according to the Bible, saw from a distance on the mountain before his first revelation. Why is it a symbol of peace? Because the bush burns but it is not consumed. The bush does not extinguish the fire, but neither does the fire consume the bush. In other words, the essence of peace is the ability of opposites to coexist so that the prophecy on top of the mountain may be heard. The burning bush is an important symbol to keep in mind in the toughest moments of conflict. It suggests that true wisdom is revealed on high, perhaps in the heights of our consciousness.

Re-Imagination

There is one final role of imagination, and that is what can be called re-imagination. When conflict is deep and damage has been done, it is hard to leave the past behind in terms of our imagination. It is also important to re-imagine the past to learn from what we and others have done wrong. Imagining a different future should never be a pretext for ignoring the past. It simply does not work, in terms of healing conflict, to ignore pain. We have to see how all the trouble began and imagine at each stage what might have prevented the next stage of the conflict, or what alternatives were available at the time. We then need to imagine what will happen if we or our opponents do things differently. We can learn to take the painful human experience of regret and turn it into a valuable step along the journey of healing.

For example, I have a friend, Joseph Montville, one of the pioneers in the field of conflict resolution, who crafted a project called Reviving the Memory of Moorish Spain. Joe began this project while directing a program on diplomacy at the Center for Strategic and International Studies in Washington, D.C. His goal was to acknowledge the pain and suffering that have gone on due to various religious wars, but also to remember that the relationship *was* different at one time. Moorish Spain in the eleventh century enjoyed an unprecedented era of healthy Jewish-Muslim-Christian relations, and Joe believes that this precedent could form the cultural basis for a better future. Good memories deserve an honored place in the stories we tell about our past. This is as true of civilizations and nations as it is of families. There is a human tendency to reference the good times only after there is a tragedy, but these memories can form the building blocks of healing.

There are so many creative ways to use imagination to help heal conflicts, both in the lives of nations and in the lives of individuals. The key is to release this creative human energy and make it a critical step in our evolution away from hatred and destructive fighting. Cultivating a positive imagination leads to knowing what to do and how to speak, the final stages of the healing process.

STEP SEVEN: DO

The Transformational Power of Deeds and Gestures

Deeds and words, Do and Speak, are the most important and final steps to healing the wounds of conflict. In a certain sense they have been with us all along as we've learned about the other steps because there is no real way to heal conflict without words and deeds. This step asks you to take everything that you've learned about your inner life and everything that you've been able to observe about the people around you and put it all into the single most powerful way we humans express ourselves: through our deeds. We begin with deeds because what we do has such power to undo the harm that has been done, often where words are inadequate to the task.

DO: TO TAKE ACTIONS IN YOUR LIFE THAT FLOW NATURALLY FROM THE WISDOM YOU HAVE ACQUIRED IN THE PREVIOUS STEPS.

A deed is like words in motion, or a dramatic statement—it speaks volumes. Though they may be full of potential risks and disappointments, the actions you take as a result of the Eight Steps allow you to learn from others' reactions how to heal conflicts and build healthy new relationships.

The key to success in this step is being persistent in your actions, which should include positive ethical deeds, gestures that have deep meaning, and thoughtful actions intended to transform relationships. Taking action nurtures an innate respect that we have for ourselves and others. We pay enormous attention to gestures that are made to us, much more than to words, because every action that we take in life is also a symbol of who and what we are. Symbolic deeds are essential ways of communicating with each other, of speaking without words, precisely because a symbol is so rich that it says far more than we could convey in speaking.

Dealing with Loved Ones

Madeleine was a member of one of my previous congregations. When she started to show the early signs of a fatal disease, unfortunately the time came for her children to make decisions about her living situation. Two of Madeleine's children, Sylvia and Bill, felt strongly that their mother needed to move into a nursing facility, as her life had become more and more difficult at home. Something had to be done, and they were struggling to make a collective decision about the right course of action. Her life was drawing to a close, and they lived far away. They thought it best that she got professional care, which is generally an ethical course of action in such cases. There were, of course, serious costs involved. On its face, assuming everyone wanted to be fair, the problem of how to share the expenses would be relatively straightforward. Bill is a successful accountant, Sylvia is a partner in a major law firm, and Ann, the other child, who is a homemaker, is married to a relatively wealthy businessman. Nonetheless, the siblings found themselves in a bitter and difficult conflict over what to do. It seems that many issues were clouding their ability to come to terms with the right action for the situation.

Part of the problem was that everyone had a different idea of what *should* be done, including Madeleine herself. Many conflicts emerge precisely at the stage of taking action, and that is where all the steps that we have studied until now should inform decisions about action. In this case, Sylvia believed strongly her mother ought to go into the "best possible" assisted-living center, and she felt that the siblings should share the cost equally. Bill felt that the cost should be shared according to who had the most money, and he resented the fact that he, the poorest of the three, would have to pay the same amount as Sylvia. Ann, on the other hand, who was closest to Madeleine, believed her mother should stay with her at her home, which was close by. But Ann wanted the others to share the financial burden of this option. Ann was prepared to pay the price emotionally for round-the-clock care, but the other siblings were suspicious and doubtful of Ann's plan. It rankled them in ways they could not easily explain.

The situation had become increasingly difficult despite the fact that everyone acknowledged a decision needed to be made quickly. And yet Ann and Sylvia, who used to spend Thanksgiving together every year, barely spoke, and Sylvia was upset over Bill's views. Over the next six months the situation deteriorated further. Ann brought in a social worker to speak to her siblings, a woman who echoed her views, but Sylvia stormed out of one meeting and Ann's attempt at rational compromise failed. Madeleine's condition continued to deteriorate, and still no solution was in sight.

Why this conflict was so difficult to solve required extensive examination. The siblings disagreeing on what to do was not problematic in and of itself; rather, a shared process of figuring out a course of action takes time and negotiation. Often we make the best decisions as we banter and argue with others, struggling to come up with a good plan of action. Sometimes it can take a bit of conflict, a genuine intellectual argument, to force us to think outside the box. At work many people enjoy debating the different issues that are of direct concern to peers as well as supervisors, and even when this debate becomes emotional and difficult, the parties involved can usually see that the process is helping the entire group come to a more thoughtful decision. Creativity and originality can be interesting by-products of conflict in healthy situations. But the conflict faced by this family was not really about what should be done for Madeleine. It was instead about hidden emotions, about the past, about unfairness; it was really about buried grievances. For this reason there was no easy solution.

Even if, by a magical process, a clear answer could be determined as to what would be best for Madeleine, the conflict might not end there. In fact, it was possible that one or more of the three siblings, Sylvia, Bill, or Ann, actually enjoyed prolonging the conflict on some level. Madeleine was in a certain sense a pawn in a chess game between the three, a game that each one found convenient for different reasons. Even that idea—that a participant in a conflict was gaining something from the conflict itself—would not make a solution hard to find if the participants admitted this was the case. However, when I talked to the three they each told me they thought the conflict was painful and difficult and they really wanted to end it, so long as that involved Madeleine receiving proper care. Yet their actions continually contradicted this assertion.

This sense of intractability, of a conflict frozen in time, with a life of its own, is familiar to me. I have seen the same pattern again and again in my peace work in the Middle East and in other trouble spots. As with any other destructive conflict, I immediately recognized how hard it would be to bring it toward solution.

Bill took a courageous step when he decided that the

best course of action was to call a family meeting in which he would be very honest about all of his feelings. He hoped this would spur his siblings on to a similar level of honesty. In other words, Bill combined in an artful way a process of taking action with honest conversation and communication.

I was not present at any of the family's meetings, but I heard from Bill the results of a major family summit that had been convened to decide what would happen with Madeleine. Bill had asked that only family members be present (no social workers), and Bill had encouraged his sisters to talk openly about their feelings and frustrations. Bill told me he began the meeting explaining to his sisters how he had felt during the intense period in which they argued about Madeleine. He told them how he had often been jealous of Ann for her closeness to his mother and how he had at times resented Sylvia's financial success. He explained that what he really wanted was what was best for his mother and he was prepared to make a considerable financial sacrifice and not direct what happened to her, so long as it was in her best interests. He explained that he had realized that all three had been ignoring Madeleine's own position, and even when they spoke to her and relayed her thoughts back to the others, her real feelings didn't seem clear.

The sisters agreed with this line of thinking and asked Madeleine what she really wanted, promising that they would not react in anger or any other emotion no matter what she said. It turned out that Madeleine did not want to live with Ann and was afraid of upsetting her by telling her this. She said she felt she would be too much of a burden on Ann. She also wanted to live in a facility that would have activities and events; she worried that if she lived with Ann she might end up watching television all day. In fact, Madeleine had already visited several facilities and had one in mind.

The family did not immediately settle the issue of which sibling will contribute what amount to their mother's expenses, but now that one of the major issues in contention had been solved, and healthy communication restored, Bill was optimistic that the details would work themselves out. The most important development was that the actions taken would now focus primarily on Madeleine herself. Her engagement with what needed to be done not only empowered her, it also led to the leadership of the entire family in their need to take a joint course of action.

The next step for the family, corresponding to the last of the Eight Steps, Speak, should involve a round of apologies for the ways in which they had hurt each other. Such words not only help put to rest the current conflict, they often transform the relationships, bringing those involved to a new level of close relations. Even if the apologies are partial, with individuals taking only some of the blame for a situation, the act itself can be contagious, prompting a new cycle of good relations, ethical courses of action, and conciliatory gestures. This would be particularly healing for the family, which would soon have to cope with the loss of their mother.

Taking Decisive Action at Life's Turning Points

Doing something to rectify a problem situation after following the Eight Steps is a powerful way of shaking off the trauma of conflict. In this way this step is not only essential for effectively reaching out to adversaries, it is essential for our own recovery from conflict.

For me, the things that I regret the most and that I am most traumatized by are the times when I was paralyzed, when I did not take action to deal with my problems but instead ran away. By contrast, the times in my life when I worked hard to understand a troubling situation, even while making significant mistakes, do not come up often as memories that haunt me.

A powerful example is my relationship with my father. After years of coldness between us, I realized that the only way to heal the wounds of the past was for me to get involved in my father's favorite activities, such as cooking and getting some sun out on our porch. There were times that I had said things that really hurt him; in fact, many people hurt my father with words. My intent and hope was to reverse the effects of whatever offense he may have taken at my statements. But he seemed so uncomfortable and easily embarrassed by raising personal issues through conversation, and it was his custom to deny that there was any problem. If I had persisted in conversation I may have offended him even more, as I did on a few occasions.

My father had the power to be conciliatory, but his genius at reconciliation was nowhere to be found in words;

rather, it could be seen in his symbolic actions and ethical deeds. He loved saying he was sorry through physical affection and warmth, through hearty greetings, through big, specially prepared meals, surprising and freely offered "snacks" (which were the size of dinners), and big, oversized greeting cards on special days that said through symbol and word what he could not say by himself. The cards with so many written words seemed absurdly large, as if to make up for the words he could not speak.

I remember so many times in all the years that I spent with my father that he almost never apologized to me with words when he knew that he had hurt me or frightened me. Instead he deliberately and simply cooked me a soup, or made me a fabulous steak, or put his hand on the nape of my neck in the synagogue as we sat together. Like many people, my father simply felt too inadequate with words, or was too overcome by emotion to deal with the spoken word. But good deeds were his chosen path of communication for those who were ready to hear his way of speaking.

Again, doing and speaking are somewhat dependent on each other. Because speaking honestly and directly was not my father's strong point, I learned over time to feel the authenticity of his gestures right at the center of my body. In the world of action my father felt more confidence, having experimented for a lifetime with right and wrong symbolic actions to others. He had within him a wealth of both successes and terrible failures on this front, people he had injured with his actions and people who loved him because of his gestures.

He had a full repertoire of good deeds that mattered to him and to those of us who loved him, such as cooking hearty soups when you needed it most, sharing great moments in film, making Saturday traditional meals for guests, sending oversized cards of love on special occasions, and simple caresses, but in the world of the spoken word he had little experience. At first I found it maddening, and then eventually I came to appreciate its depth. Taking my father's lead, I eventually used my actions to transform our relationship.

I took special interest in cooking with him, as did my other siblings. I went out of my way to make him feel good physically, with warm blankets, good socks, and fresh air. I made sure that the aides we brought in payed special attention to the quality of his showers and general grooming; he appreciated that. I went out of my way to sit with him on many occasions, watching great drama on television and talking about the heroic actors or the beautiful actresses. He loved that. More than anything, in those later years I passively accepted with gratitude everything he cooked for me, diet or no diet. It meant too much to him to refuse, and it was the one place of empowerment that defined his best intentions in life. He came from a family of nurturers, people who took immense pleasure in feeding the hungry, and much as I was personally frustrated with issues of overeating or lack of communication in other ways, I knew that this was a deeply positive experience for him and for me, that the moment for it was fleeting and needed to be seized before it would all end.

Whether it is the special moments in the life of families or in the life of communities, our task is to seize the opportunity to do good and nurturing deeds that lead to healing. For individuals as well as feuding nations, the challenge is to figure out the correct transformative actions to take in addressing a conflict. Here are some general principles to consider.

- Our actions should be an outgrowth of what we have learned from the other steps in the Eight Step process. Now that we have identified our feelings and understand the conflict, and, most importantly, now that we have realized (in Be) the ways we, or the group we are part of, contribute to the conflict, we can begin to imagine actions that can remedy the hurt.
- Our actions should be carefully attuned to the specific circumstances of each of our relationships and conflicts—the more we understand about the root of the conflict, the more directed our action can be.
- As we choose our actions of Do, we should draw upon our greatest strengths, the things we do best, and build from them a course of action. We must constantly ask ourselves, What do we do best? What can we do well enough to achieve a solution?
- The actions required at this stage should not just have symbolic value for our adversaries. They must also, like the slave march, have symbolic value and transformative power *for ourselves*. We must make efforts to both heal and be healed.

- Before acting, carefully consider if a certain deed, though well intentioned, could make matters worse or communicate the wrong message. This requires referring back to what you've learned in the previous steps, and a level of humility.
- Our actions will work only if they are authentic, not concessions made in a half-hearted spirit. If we have been in long-standing conflict in the office or in a family, a single act of generosity and self-sacrifice will not undo years of resentment unless it becomes an ongoing gesture that has transformational power over us as well as our adversaries. In a sense, the magic of *doing* must change us to be effective on others.

This step, although challenging, when informed by the work done in the previous steps has the added advantage of helping us define who we are in relationship to others, leading to a possibly profound fulfillment of our aspirations. My father, for instance, spent his early years trying to prove his manhood through physical strength. But there is no greater or more manly gift he ever gave me than the gift of simple affection.

As a kosher butcher and the son of a kosher butcher, his biceps were enormous from lifting heavy meats, whole sides of beef. Many decades later, when his body was old and broken, his right arm muscles were the only ones that survived the effects of a debilitating stroke. Astonishingly, his right arm was powerful till the day he died. The last thing he did for me, the last moment that I saw him, was when, with eyes closed by weakness and a semi-coma, and in a stupor of a raging and endless fever that lasted for weeks, Dad lay on his hospital bed and managed to move his right arm out toward me. I lay my head down on the hospital bed to make it easier for him to pass his hand through my hair, back and forth, back and forth, my face buried in the white hospital sheets, shuddering in awe because he was supposed to be unconscious. That was strength, that was incredible power, that was an act of manhood. After life-long conflicts, which can be so bewildering, it never ceases to amaze me how simple and elegant the gestures of healing often are.

Take Action
Before Conflict Becomes Destructive

Taking decisive and meaningful action is not only important for healing old wounds or managing a conflict that is ongoing, but also in anticipation of conflict, as a way of short-circuiting a situation that is likely to become destructive. This is especially true in long-term family relations. Children are so utterly dependent that if parents show favoritism toward one child or another early on, this could cause enormous anxiety. The competition for attention is constant at a certain age, and I am not sure it ever disappears entirely. It is as if when we are on the receiving end of love or attention we are paralyzed by it, dependent on it entirely.

Wise action, however, can forestall this anxiety. Parents

should try to get their children to compete proactively in good ways, to compete in acts of goodness. For example, no matter how much love we shower on our two daughters, on any given day, left to themselves and their own insecurities, they will start vying for our attention in not-so-healthy ways, such as fighting for lap time, for who gets to sit next to Mommy, for who gets to wash their hands first—it can be maddening. But when *we* set the agenda and make cleaning up, for example, into a good deed and an exciting activity, or running and jumping as a healthy activity, then they are on their way to working together and helping each other.

The competition and uncertainties of security among children never really disappear with age or maturity, as far as I can tell. Adult children seem plagued by the same concerns as they deal with aging parents. As I look back on the last years of my father's life I remember some family struggles over how to best take care of him, different philosophies of dealing with his bad habits or physical challenges, but I distinctly remember becoming closer to my wonderful siblings in that period. When Terri came to visit she sometimes brought Dad exactly the foods that I did not think he should be eating, but I never said a word, and in the end I really learned to appreciate what Terri was really doing. She was making him happy and loved at the end of his life, and we were well past the point anyway where diet could have really reversed his physical condition. He set the tone—he was totally uninterested in dieting but definitely enjoyed being appreciated. She took his cues and ran with them, and I respect her for doing that.

Competition in goodness among rivals is the dream result of this step. Defining yourself in a positive way creates a spiral of good relations that yield surprisingly powerful forms of reconciliation. It puts the lie to the notion that competition always creates destructive conflict, because it is the goodness of doing for others that creates bonds of friendship and respect despite inevitable disagreements.

This is true also in the larger arena of political and ethnic divisions. I recall my meeting with a group of young Jordanian men at a retreat high up in the mountains of Switzerland, at an event sponsored yearly by the group Initiatives of Change. I knew that the Jordanians were at the conference and was at first apprehensive about bumping into them.

I was out on the porch overlooking the mountains, along with many other people, I believe at teatime. The young men came up to me quite abruptly, all smiles, and introduced themselves. The problem is that they thought that I was someone else, a translator who resembled me! Nevertheless, the ice was broken, and I seized the opportunity. They did not shirk from the encounter either, although it quickly took on a more tense tone.

They wanted to know many things about me, and were quite forward about it. They grilled me, in fact, whereas I tried to keep the initial encounters nonchalant, with a greater focus on interpersonal exchange. Finally, we agreed to meet later. At the meeting we sat at a round table with most of them facing me. I asked personal questions, about their lives in Jordan and their career aspirations, and about television programs from Jordan that I had seen broadcast in Israel. I tried to keep it light, but their questions to me continued to be political in nature as they launched into questions about what I thought about Israel: Should Israel have the right to prevent the Palestinians from forming a state of their own? Should Israelis be allowed to construct settlements in the Occupied Territories? Why did a democracy like Israel refuse to treat Palestinians equally?

It did not seem to matter that I lived in America and was not Israeli. Still, I understood how much they felt the intensity of the conflict, and I surmised that most of them were of Palestinian origin and had direct family memories of trauma. I could see that these political conversations were going to end up with not much resolved, however, as is the case most of the time. I found myself in a quandary about how to engage them.

My time in Switzerland at Initiatives of Change's mountain retreat in Caux became a fairly regular summer event for me, and it always stimulated in me reflections about the nature of conflict and healing. This time was no different. The Alps, the diversity of people from all over the world, and the prayerful atmosphere always made me reflect on the deepest matters in my life and the future of humanity. People came from every continent, representing every race and religion, and it transformed my thinking. I resolved that in this situation with the young Jordanians I needed to be mindful of everything I did near these young men, every action that I took. I saw the opportunity to take some risks and to make a statement with the most subtle of my deeds.

The first thing I "did," however, was to prepare myself with lessons learned from the other steps. For example, I *imagined* what these young men expected of me, what picture they might have had in mind of how I would behave. Clearly they were angry at Israel, and I guessed that the only Israelis they had ever seen were soldiers, possibly at the border between Israel and Jordan or on television. Their initial questions led me to believe that they had little experience themselves with Israelis. I imagined that they expected me to treat them badly because that is what they assumed Jews would do. Frankly, I had to deal with the hurt that came from that realization. I thought to myself, "Why should I be judged for the actions of others? Why are they generalizing about everyone on the Israeli side?" But the discipline of healing conflicts with others requires us to go through the Eight Steps repeatedly in our minds, especially during such difficult encounters, and it finally occurred to me that *doing* was a priority this time.

I decided to act exactly the opposite of what they might expect of me, in an almost exaggerated fashion. I had an advantage: I was older than they were, which gave me insight they didn't have access to. From experience I knew that honor and shame were a core issue of the Arab-Israeli conflict, despite what diplomats and politicians may tell us. Every time they approached me as a group I did something to honor one of them. I sprung up out of my chair as soon as they approached and rushed to greet them first. I offered to get them an extra chair, showing respect. This shocked them for a number of reasons, including the fact that I was older and a cleric of a religion that they associated negatively with conflict.

The young men instinctively returned the gestures, as people so often do. They quickly invited me to be part of their voluntary team that worked in the kitchen of the retreat center. We set up for dinner together, and I asked them to teach me how to do everything. This too honored them.

By the end of the conference we had developed an unusual level of kinship. In fact, one of the young men spoke with such admiration of me in a public gathering that I was moved, and I went up and publicly embraced him. The audience was astounded, and so was I! I did not expect or plan to do that. Just as bad behavior and actions have a nasty habit of creating spirals of destructive conflict, so too powerful actions of healing, honor, and compassion have a life of their own, and often lead to unexpected and blessed places. This is the power of *doing* as one of the most important of the Eight Steps.

Gestures to Heal the Past

A number of us at the retreat in Switzerland that same year had been talking for days about events long ago, in World War II. The retreat center, located in the tiny village of Caux, actually had housed thousands of Jewish refugees from all over Europe who barely escaped with their lives from Nazi-occupied Europe. Now we sat and socialized in a large room that had been the sleeping quarters for hundreds of families who had just barely escaped the killing machine that was the Holocaust.

Right below our beautiful retreat center high up in the Alps, we could see what had been the border between Switzerland and Nazi-occupied France. At that border thousands of families were turned away and went to their deaths—about forty thousand Jewish men, women, and children. The Swiss guards would not let them in.

The reality of that terrible event was front and center at the time in numerous discussions going on regarding Swiss actions during World War II. It was a raw subject between Swiss people themselves as well, particularly in the wake of revelations about how some Swiss banks had unduly taken advantage of the victims.

I found myself engaged in many conversations, as I was perceived as a Jew with intense feelings about the behavior of Europe during the Holocaust, but also as a person who was used to peacemaking and bridge building. Swiss people felt that they could be frank with me about how angry they were at their own country, whereas other Swiss folks felt comfortable defending their parents' generation, and the practical dilemmas of dealing with the Nazi war machine, without fear that I would accuse them of anti-Semitism. I treasured that role, as painful as it was from time to time, especially because the people I was in conversation with were so wonderful. At the same time, there were others no longer alive now who made me exceedingly angry, who I felt were guilty of the kind of prejudices that led to the Holocaust.

We all went home from the summer conferences, but conversations continued. Finally, after months of dealing with these issues through words, it seemed time for something to be done. But what? The tragedy had happened over fifty years ago; the victims were long dead. It was proposed that we should somehow commemorate what had happened near the resort—a monument and a tree, someone suggested, that would acknowledge the refugees who had survived because they were let into the country and those who did not because they were kept out. From now on this monument would become a part of the story of Caux, and it would be a symbol of honor, acknowledgement, and the birth of reconciliation symbolized by the living tree. Coming up with this plan of action was something whose time at Caux had come. There were many discussions over the wording of the plaque and how it could acknowledge both those refugees who made it to Caux and those who could not get over the border. A memorial ceremony was then conceived and I was asked to officiate. Everyone walked down to the plot of land where the new tree was planted overlooking Lake Geneva, and I said some traditional prayers for the dead. The plaque was also unveiled near the tree. The ceremony meant more to me than I can say.

Something extraordinary happened after that. I remember sitting on the veranda overlooking Lake Geneva, and a man I had never met before came up to me and asked if he could join me. He said nothing but his name, and then he looked at me intently. He had a serious, stoic look of meaningful intensity not uncommon in the Swiss. He said, "I was a guard on that border." The remarkable thing is that this was all he could say to me. No apologies, no explanations, nothing. He was literally speechless as he peered deeply into my eyes with such a remorseful look on his face. In that context, and knowing his culture fairly well, I took his action of coming up to me as an act of acknowledgment.

Here, in this moment, was the power of *doing* revealed. I felt at peace as this man sat with me—in some ways even more at peace than at the tree ceremony, for he had brought history alive, his presence making the connection between now and then: the past was no myth, my anger at the lack of acknowledgment of history was not just a personal gripe, and the ceremony was not just a cordial tip of the hat to my personal problems with history. This was real—he made it real by what he did. In fact, his inability to say anything spoke clearly about how he felt. I've seen this step work the same way many times before—thoughtful action frees people from crushing silence, providing a unique opportunity for reconciliation.

Resilience and Courage

In this same place in Switzerland I remember one time being in the strange position of informally comforting and counseling a senior cleric who had barely survived the conflict in former Yugoslavia and who was witness to the worst atrocities of the war. His region was subject to a brutal occupation by murderous forces. Daily he walked past a concentration camp hearing the screams of men from his own community. He was traumatized for years after the events, and I remember listening to his story and weeping with him over the suffering and deaths of thousands of his people. At the time, this senior cleric had marshaled enormous courage to engage in attempts at reconciliation right in the middle of the horrors. He found the audacity to befriend guards of the camp, and by treating them as human beings, by forcing himself to think spiritually about them as creatures of God, he started to discover that some of them were uncomfortable with what was going on inside. In this way he was able to save a number of lives by negotiating the release of at least some of the prisoners. He engaged in powerful gestures both in order to save lives and in order to practice his faith to the best of his abilities, even as he continued to be haunted by those people whose lives he could not save.

On a beautiful summer night I sat with this Christian cleric at a Jewish Sabbath dinner prepared by some Swiss friends. We sat, along with more than thirty friends—Jewish, Christian, and Muslim—late into the night. So as not to spoil the festive spirit of the dinner, he and I sat closely together and spoke quietly to each other, through a translator, in hushed words. I have lived so long with detailed knowledge of the Holocaust, always ambivalent about sharing it with others. I had watched films of the Holocaust and read books about it since childhood, and the Holocaust spurred my earliest concentration on violence and reconciliation. Then of course there were family memories from Europe, and the scores of relatives never heard from again, and our ancestral Jewish village erased from history by the Nazis. But that night in Caux, high up in the Swiss Alps, the Christian cleric and I spoke as if we were brothers, as if we were exploring as two clergymen the dark secrets of human nature and destiny: anguish, guilt, defiance, nightmare. We indulged memory as if it were the only thing we could do for the dead. A conservative and broken Christian cleric—a survivor—in close intimacy with a rabbi at a traditional Sabbath table, with the bread and wine before our eyes, comforting each other. Were we in the depths of hell together as we relived genocide, or were we in heaven where religious divides mean little and strangers feel as if they are at one with each other? I was in both that night. The unspeakable destructiveness of human violence was never more present for me than on that night, but the bonds of good deeds and symbolic gestures between friends made me feel as if, together, we had conquered all boundaries between religions and all barriers to healing.

This may sound like a highly unusual situation, and the kind of healing that is rare, but in all my years of work and friendships I have listened to the same kind of story from every corner of the globe. The bishop was not the only one to engage genocidal soldiers. I know of a Buddhist leader in Sri Lanka, a teacher and a friend, who talked with compassion to a man who was sent to assassinate him; a minister in

Africa, another friend, who steered child soldiers from a murderous path; and a senior Buddhist monk who lured genocidal soldiers away from their commanders in Cambodia. Each of these courageous and healing actions involved surprising gestures that treated enemies in ways that they were entirely unprepared for. It disarmed them and awoke in them a humanity that had been buried by their participation in or acquiescence to massive crimes.

These examples point out an important aspect of human nature: resilience in the face of great conflict. These people were not frozen by their fears but were able to act courageously in extreme situations. Such resilience sets the stage for recovery from the traumas of conflict, whereas paralysis in the face of danger sets the stage for long-term trauma. People who are resilient in their efforts to end conflict exemplify the transformative power of the Eight Steps.

Extraordinary circumstances bring out extraordinary human beings who teach us how to be our best in more ordinary circumstances. We come to understand beyond a shadow of a doubt that good deeds at the right moment are a healing balm like none other, and that we must reflect, each in our own circumstance, on how to exercise the power of our deeds in the search for healing.

STEP EIGHT: SPEAK

The Challenge of Dialogue and Communication

Now that we have completed seven of the Eight Steps, we can move on to what others tend to do without sufficient preparation: engage the power of words. At this point you should recognize that the words that pass between yourself and others can encourage conflict or, used with care, can help heal. The great task before us is how to achieve wondrous things with words even in the context of destructive conflicts that have hurt us personally. That's where the training of the previous seven steps will guide you.

> **SPEAK:** TO INCORPORATE THE LESSONS LEARNED IN THE PREVIOUS STEPS INTO EVERY WORD WE USE, WITH A GOAL IN MIND OF COMMUNICATING, RECONCILING, AND HEALING CONFLICTS.

Your job in Step Eight is to choose your words wisely to build bridges to deeper communication in your relationships. Even at this late stage, the truly great peacemakers—

Senator George Mitchell comes to mind—watch every single word they say. Whatever context they find themselves in, every single word is measured; every single word is designed to open up new possibilities, to present solutions rather than problems, to heal rather than damage.

So far we have learned to see how our personality and basic needs can promote conflict; to understand the nature of conflict in general and our unique conflicts in particular; to become aware of the effects of our emotional life on conflict; to listen to what our adversaries say and don't say; to observe everything about the conflict that we can see; to imagine new ways of interacting; and to engage transformative deeds to change the nature of our relationships. In this final stage we learn to speak in a healing way to our adversaries, and yet speech can have no power—it can seem empty and hollow and actually make things worse—unless it is informed by the other steps. Now we need to ask, "How can I communicate differently from the way I used to?" and "What am I going to avoid saying that I may have said previously?"

Now speech should extend from your heart to hearts of those with whom you've been in conflict.

Border Crossings

I remember being in a tense situation on a violent border. The border was backed up with traffic for miles, no one looking happy. One of the soldiers at the border caught sight of us and came running over to our little traveling group. He was short and stocky, his face flushed as he ran over to us carrying a huge weapon, always looking over his shoulder and all around him. He said, "You can't stay here, you are in danger!" I knew it was going to take us time to figure out what to do and that this man could lose his cool at any moment.

I collected myself, looked right into his eyes, smiled, then said to him, "I really appreciate your protecting us. I can see that you are worried and that this is a bad situation. The truth is that *I* am worried about what is going to happen to *you*. I wish you the best of health in this awful mess." He kept looking all around him and said to me nervously, "I don't want to be here. I would rather be on the beach with my family."

The good thing is that I had got him to talk just for a moment about himself. I had established relations with him quickly in a bad situation. This somewhat defused his sense of urgency, and it gave us the time to figure out what to do in the meantime. That was my short-term aim—the soothing words I used that spoke to his heart were the key.

In our day-to-day lives, many experiences do not allow us to engage all of the previous steps—or even some of them—before we are faced with an explosive situation where we must speak. That was the situation we found ourselves in at the border—with absolutely no preparation and no prior knowledge of any of the people involved. At such times it becomes necessary to at least keep all the other steps of healing in our consciousness and in our feelings. At the very least the awareness of these steps, and the lessons that they embody, will give us a way to engage others with greater thoughtfulness and care.

The encounter between the soldier and me is an interesting case to study. I first thought about my own safety and excessive fears that I was having at that moment (Be). Quickly, I assessed the situation and identified what response was called for (Understand). I carefully listened to every word the soldier was saying and looked for a possible opening (Hear). I then evaluated his behavior in the context of the situation, the danger from the crowds, and his relation to our group (See); I also saw how the soldier's concerns were exaggerated as to how much the group and I were creating an incident in a hostile environment; I saw that it was he who was generating the most hostility. I put myself in his shoes (Imagine), thinking about what he might be going through, which in turn helped me to think of the right words to speak.

Northern Ireland

Although much of my work has focused on the Middle East, I have on occasion worked in other crisis areas, including Africa and Northern Ireland. The Northern Ireland conflict involves wounds of bitterness and hatred that go back centuries. As I often engage groups of people at community gatherings, this has given me the chance to observe people struggling with their words as they argued about terrible tragedies in the past and the present but also strove to communicate in new ways. When I visited Northern Ireland, I went to meet with members of a new, interesting community group that wanted to put an end to the violence. The group was religious but nonsectarian and included Protestant and Catholic members.

I did not discuss the Eight Steps with the group members before the meeting, but it occurred to me that many of them must have spent years examining their own thoughts and feelings, trying all the while to imagine solutions. In the course of many conversations I gathered that these thoughtful, courageous people had spent much time thinking about who they were (Be), how they felt (Feel), and the conflict itself (Understand). Their attendance at the meeting of this pioneering group revealed a profound ability to visualize a different future (Imagine).

An enjoyable aspect of working in Ireland is the Irish knack for telling a story. That was certainly the case with this group, a tense meeting of Catholics and Protestants. All were committed to peacemaking, but each side brought to the meeting the historical baggage of the Troubles, as recent Irish history is referred to, and a strong, negative perception of their adversary. One young Protestant man got up and said, in effect, "My ancestors came here to this land from England, stole it, and abused the native residents. I do not know where I belong or whether I deserve to be here." This man was quite publicly asking the kind of questions that we discussed in Step One, both of himself and his religious group. By calling into question his own legitimacy, he challenged his own right to his homeland, at least temporarily. He was being honest at a profound level that is rare in interfaith dialogue.

The response this outburst drew from the crowd was perhaps equally shocking. A Catholic got up after him and said, "*Flaitulacht.*" Roughly translated, this means "Welcome to our home." The way it was explained to me, it also suggests an obligation to treat the person with special care, to make them feel as if your home is their home. If you fail to commit to the *Flaitulacht* offered, then you forfeit the rights to your own home. The Protestant gave up his right to a home, and the Catholic immediately restored it to him, but based on a completely new relationship. When I witnessed this scene, I was moved by its honesty, its hopeful drama of reconciliation, all through the use of a single word.

There is so much work left to be done in Northern Ireland, so much that still needs to be negotiated in terms of the final status of the Northern provinces. Healing on a broad social level is still in its infancy, even after thirty years of courageous efforts. Still, I left in 1998 convinced that there were many extraordinary people probing the depths of this conflict, exploring a path of healing that was bound to catch on eventually. They had begun authentic dialogue, and the relationships being created would contribute significantly to healing the larger conflict between the two communities over the course of the coming decades.

When we find ourselves in serious and continuing conflict, what we can hope to achieve and to consider a success will be those moments in which what we say or what we do has a perceivable and transformative effect on at least some of those involved. If we do this then we are contributing positively to a good much larger than ourselves. The same holds true for conflicts involving families.

Choosing and Anticipating Every Word

As we turn from these diverse examples, let's consider some general guidelines for choosing words that can help heal our conflicts.

- Choose words that mean a great deal to you but that will also mean a great deal to your adversaries.
- Train yourself to keep in mind the other Eight Steps as you choose each word.
- Anticipate emotionally and intellectually how you will respond when words are spoken back to you in response. Anticipate your reactions to kind words as well as cruel words, positive words as well as negative ones. Allow for harsh words, but keep them in perspective. Try to respond with words that speak to the heart, that bring everyone a greater level of consciousness.
- Do not use healing words unless you mean them. Dishonesty is easily detectable.
- Always accompany healing words with healing deeds and symbolic gestures. In other words, do not forget the other steps. These can be simple gestures but they must be sincere.

- Be patient with yourself and others when you or they are not ready for healing words. They will come eventually when the other steps set the stage for them, and when harsh words and deeds have exhausted themselves.

- Do not be discouraged by harsh words, and do not allow them to throw you into despair. They are, after all, just words. Reflect on whether the time is ripe for a more clever use of conversation or dialogue or to concentrate on the healing possibilities of the other Eight Steps.

- Do not allow your work to be tyrannized by time constraints in any way. Many conversations and dialogues go badly because of absurd restraints of time. Words come in their proper time and should not be forced. Do not think that every meeting must yield results and change. Just listen, watch, wait, and practice speaking with great patience and humility. Wait for your opportunity to say what must be said and then seize the moment. Then wait patiently and see what happens.

- Do not be afraid to repeat yourself when it comes to words of acknowledgment or apology. Repetition of healing words and healing deeds is essential to human growth and change. Develop the inner discipline to not be discouraged by the time and effort this takes.

- If you allow the words and deeds of others to control your sense of self, then conflict will crush you and you will not be able to heal yourself or your adversaries. Remember Step One, Be. Keep in your mind always the desire to learn how to distinguish between mistakes you have made as a person in conflict and your basic value as a person. This will give you the strength to take action and speak as a strong, confident, and honest person. Only in this way will your conversations and dialogues yield healing deeds and healing words.

Speaking in a way that can promote healing involves many experiments and failures, and we should be prepared to spend a lifetime improving this skill. People generally get better at this over time. Although destructive conflict can strike without warning, developing this ability can help us prevent and heal conflicts as they arise.

Healing Words in the Midst of War

I have had few occasions in my life to affect or interfere in the course of wars. One of the few occasions when I had the opportunity to deal face to face with truly hardcore warriors who have killed many people was a fateful visit in 2000 with Yasser Arafat, the president of the Palestinian Authority. How and why I was invited in the midst of violent confrontations between Israel and the Palestinians for a private audience is a complicated story and I will not go into it here. The point is that my partners and I saw it as an opportunity to try to effect some real change in the course of this tragic conflict. As I write this, there are still people dying every day, and this was true also when we went.

History will record that Yasser Arafat never truly made

a successful transition from guerilla leader to statesman and peacemaker. His people have suffered enormously as a result. Undoubtedly part of his failure can be blamed on Israeli treatment of the Palestinians, but there have been better examples in history of resistance leaders who seized the moral high ground. Nevertheless, Arafat was elected as leader of his people. I felt it incumbent upon myself to seize every opportunity to introduce new gestures and new relationships that could stem the cycle of violence.

It was the spring of 2001, six months into the latest Intifada, when I met with Arafat again. I presented myself mainly as a rabbi because he has a certain openness to clerics, and I had managed to be taken quite seriously at high levels of his government. All of us in the room that day spoke at great length about our religious visions of the Holy Land and of a Middle East that would be unencumbered by borders. A colleague of mine led the way as we indulged our imaginations. In so doing we created some interesting bonds, as I describe in Step Six. Our ideal visions bypassed all the political, ethnic, and military challenges that divided us. I explained in Imagine how important these flights of fantasy can be to trust-building, which in turn can set the stage for the transformations of conflicted relationships.

I told the Palestinian leadership gathered that day that it was an ancient Jewish tradition to engage in comforting mourners and that I mourned with them over their losses in the preceding months, especially of their children. I laid no blame on anyone, and I did not discuss responsibility, neither theirs nor that of the Israelis. I kept my judgments to myself on these matters, and I merely expressed sorrow at the loss of life. They were visibly moved by this because they knew that as I spoke these words I was engaged in a religious act of my tradition designed not to attack, not to judge, but to comfort them. The surprise on their faces was noticeable.

I took a chance and went even further. I saw how much easier it was to speak to Arafat in symbolic language, especially if it honored him in some way. I leaned close to him, and I said, "I want to share something with you from my ancient rabbis. They said, 'The world survives due to three things: truth, justice, and peace.'" Then I leaned even closer to him, looked straight into his eyes, and said, "Another rabbi in the Talmudic sacred literature added, 'Where there is no justice there can never be peace.'" Here I looked at him with some sympathy. But then I added the last quotation: "But where there is no peace there will never be justice." He looked at me intently. He had smiled many times before, but he was not smiling now. He looked at me for a while, and then said, "This is important."

Arafat is extremely sharp, and he knew that I was speaking to him, heart to heart, through symbolic language. In the first part of the quotation from sacred literature, I was acknowledging as a Jew the injustices that his people had suffered. But in the second part of the sentence I was completely rejecting the means with which he was choosing to struggle, and had always chosen. I was quoting ancient sources to tell him that his way of fighting could never bring peace or justice to himself or his people.

The conversation went on for a time about other things, but Arafat kept silent, looking at me intently, and I at him. Then suddenly he turned to me and said, "You know, when I was a boy I used to go among the Jewish men at the Western Holy Wall who were praying, and I would say my own prayers there together with their prayers." It is not often that my mouth drops, but it did at that moment. The Western Wall, in the Old City of Jerusalem, is at the core of the conflict, the most deeply contested site with one of the oldest mosques in the world, the third holiest site in Islam, and the ruins of the two most holy temples in Judaism right underneath. Many religious leaders in the Palestinian community were claiming at the time that Jews had no place there, that it had no historical connection to the Jewish people, and that the attachment of the Jews to the spot was all part of a Zionist myth and conspiracy. But here he was acknowledging exactly what they were denying, right after I had spoken.

I realized that he was returning the gesture of the spoken word right back to me. I had honored him, acknowledged his people's losses, and he returned the gesture by using carefully chosen words to acknowledge Jerusalem as a sacred Jewish place. I believe that what happened in that room on that day was due to the powerful work of the word, the right words, words that honor, words that comfort, and words that heal.

It was a small victory, but that is exactly what you build upon in bitter conflicts, one small victory at a time.

The next day was the first day in six months of fighting that Arafat publicly announced that people on his side should not be attacking innocent Jewish civilians. I will never know whether our visit and the words we exchanged had any relation to that announcement, and I also fully acknowledge that this was a small drop in an ocean of destructive conflict. Arafat reversed himself many times subsequently and supported terrorist acts, which he called martyrdom, while Israeli retaliations and collective punishments would become ever more severe. We have evidence from friends that the effect of those visits was profound, and that they could have helped decrease the severity of the conflict, but only if they had been followed up with dozens of exchanges with a similar spirit by Israelis or government representatives on both sides. But that never happened. No government in the world has understood, to this day, the importance of healing this conflict with the approach that we, among many others, tried. They fail to understand how much matters of the heart, such as honor, shame, outrage, despair, and injury, drive people to actions that they know are destructive. They fail to understand the practical effects of addressing these matters of the heart, and how they can lead to powerful gestures, imagined possibilities, and effective negotiations. With all of their military strength and financial prowess, most government leaders are cowardly when it comes to the realm of human emotions and gestures. That is where they need our help the most. We had no victory on that fateful day in terms of the larger war, but we had a smaller victory in terms of the human relationships in that room, because no one left unmoved.

War is such an overwhelming human tragedy, with so many contributing causes that it is naïve to think that mere words can change everything, and I would never want to leave the reader with that impression. On the other hand, it is foolish to deny, as so many policy makers do, the contribution of well-chosen words to setting relationships in either a good direction or a destructive direction. The inability to acknowledge the independent power and importance of conciliatory words, for example, has led to many outrageous exchanges of words in this and many other Middle Eastern conflicts.

I remember going to those meetings with Arafat with a fantastic amount of fear inside. Every moment I was in that building I felt a mixture of physical fear, revulsion, uncertainty, even guilt. After doing much listening and observation over the course of the hours we spent there, and going through the Eight Steps in my mind, again and again, the bad feelings lessened but did not disappear.

It was only after I spoke what was in my heart that all of the bad feelings turned into calm resignation. I had gone through years of living with this conflict, outraged by its waste of human life, but at that moment, after speaking the truth, I felt a calm come over me, as if in that room, sitting on that couch, with rabbi friends on one side and these military figures on the other, I had spoken to myself, to my own heart, and I had said to myself finally, "Now you have done everything you could to stop the killing."

When the speaking is finally done, after the other steps, it should leave you with a sense of calm and completion— this too is an essential stage of healing, no matter what happens in the larger conflict. This step, like the others, is not about controlling everything in the world around you because no human being has that power. It is about doing everything in *your* power to change destiny and then leaving it up to fate or God to control the rest. Healing does not come from absolute control over others or over history; that is an illusion. It comes from knowing yourself well enough to make yourself into a vehicle of healing and then humbly accepting what comes.

The Power of Ritual

One of my favorite healing moments happened during a meeting at my home between leaders from both sides of the Middle East conflict. Most of the participants were politically moderate, but all were in a highly charged state due to the continuing bloodshed and the recent trauma of 9/11. Under these circumstances, I felt quite certain that the most important thing I could do would be to overwhelm the circumstances with deeds and gestures. I made the meeting at my home, and I made sure that my mother and my little children were there to welcome and talk to all the guests. I made sure that the foods would appeal to both tastes, and I served this food myself. I chose not to hide various books on my bookshelf whose titles stemmed from Jewish tradition, but everyone was greeted personally, and everyone was introduced to the others, one by one.

I believe strongly in the power of ritual, including ritualized speech. What happened at my house that day is that we intuitively organized a kind of ceremony, where words of honor and welcome were exchanged. As people were coming in I steered the conversation toward family. We spoke of our children. A wise psychologist friend of mine seized the moment to point out that her children were going to the same schools as the Saudis' children, and the words tripped out of one Arab gentleman, inviting my friend and her children to his home. She moved closer to them and engaged them in further discussion about family.

I will never forget the powerful way in which one man connected with this American audience. One of his grown children was in Manhattan on that terrible day when three thousand people died in an instant. He, like many of the more modern Saudis, is proud of his children's liberal education and of their cosmopolitan worldliness, especially that of his daughters. He told us of how panicked he was for hours, unable to reach his child by phone in Manhattan. With that one story, about his pride in his children and his suffering on that day when millions of the rest of us suffered, it was impossible for anyone in my living room to generalize badly about all Saudis.

After the Saudi men spoke, each of the twenty-five others present introduced themselves, their professions, and the ways in which they had worked over the years on interfaith matters or on coexistence in the Middle East. We did not realize as we planned this event the impact that it would have on these guests to see a roomful of people who in one way or another had dedicated so much of their lives to peace. I opened the floor for questions and comments with the proviso that this was the *beginning* of a relationship, that nothing would be solved here and now, but that we must begin.

The questions were pointed and direct. Some of the questions were tough and rather accusatory. Other questions were plaintive and confessional, admitting hurt and confusion in the current climate. It was obvious that this was just the beginning of such discussions, and it was never our intent for the discussion to get down to negotiations or solutions. Those would come later if the relationship were to be given a chance to develop.

What Step Eight had accomplished here was a greater level of respect, honor, sympathy, and kinship. It marked the beginning of serious intellectual exchange. Many in the Jewish group expressed the pain and disappointment of recent violence and injuries, but really shone in their capacity to use dialogue as an opportunity to strengthen understanding of complex problems. Most people in that room demonstrated remarkably well the requisite skills of listening and speaking with a subtle combination of intelligent criticism and openness to new possibilities. All in all, Speak was utilized by people on two sides of a difficult divide as a bridge rather than a barrier, as a way of relating rather than as a way of destroying relations, as a way of honoring rather than humiliating, as a vehicle to begin more discussions rather than as a weapon to destroy them.

Taking the Time to Talk

A final observation: One of the most important things missing from modern urban life—and this is true increasingly on every continent of the globe—is time. The loss of time is a great price we are paying because time is critical for healing.

Indigenous people in many parts of the world have developed over the centuries healing ceremonies that last for weeks, even months, where people work out their conflicts. Everyone involved in the conflict, including bystanders, speaks until they have said everything and anything that comes to mind, while everyone else patiently listens. Emotions can run high, and it can be difficult to listen to the views of an adversary that one strongly disagrees with, but because everyone knows in these indigenous conversations that they will be able to speak for as long as they want, the sense of anger and frustration at being silenced is removed. We may get angry at others talking too much primarily because we feel it will take our own voice away, our chance to speak our point of view; we also may feel that with the views others are expressing, the "truth" of a situation will never become clear.

Extensive conversation with no time limit relieves this frustrating feeling, and this in turn offers the chance for not only speaking to succeed, but also hearing and understanding. I would argue that imagination is also encouraged because the more time people have to speak together, the more they are given to sharing their nightmares and dreams in an open and honest way, which in turn leads to creative joint dreaming of new possibilities. A lack of time consciousness was crucial to some of my most successful engagements in peacemaking.

Perhaps such open conversations, facilitated by senior persons of great wisdom, as is done in indigenous communities, could be incorporated into forward-thinking businesses, community centers, schools, and places of worship. The key would be the commitment to let the conversation go on for as long as necessary for everyone's voice to be heard, even if this takes months or longer. The value of this would be the speaking and listening itself, not as some task to be accomplished but as an opportunity for healing.

PART TWO

THE

EIGHT

STEPS

APPLIED

WORK

The Eight Steps in Making a Living

The workplace is a kind of community, and the quality of our relationships with members of that community is obviously very important to our sense of security and self-worth. We want to be in an exciting environment that is both challenging and supportive, that pushes us to our highest potential but that is also there for us when we falter. But the human need for community has necessary limits within the workplace. Sometimes what is good for community may hamper production, and vice versa. It may be great to have a weeklong fair that celebrates arts and crafts made by workers after a winter of hard production schedules. What if, on the other hand, end-of-year reports indicate that unless the company achieves a certain level of productivity by June, investors will start pulling out? Productivity is in constant

WORK: INTEGRATE THE EIGHT STEPS INTO YOUR DAY-TO-DAY WORK RELATIONSHIPS IN SUCH A WAY THAT CONFLICTS ARE PREVENTED, MINIMIZED, AND HEALED WHEN THEY DO OCCUR.

tension with other needs and it is easy for this tension to create conflict.

Another challenge is that there are great variations among workers. Some of us as workers may want more independence, while others want more guidance. Everyone wants dignity, respect, and tangible rewards for their hard work. We also have unique expectations based on our background and psychology. Some of us want to work with our peers, side by side, while others are especially competitive. Some of us do not want the attention that success brings, or a high profile, because we feel that those who fly high fall fast and hard; what we want instead is long-term security. Some of us have few ambitions at work because our heart lies in fulfillment at home or in other forms of productivity.

All of this makes it hard for colleagues to satisfy one another's expectations—a prescription for conflict. But these workplace challenges need not turn into destructive conflicts. If we address these complex situations with positive internal practices and external actions aimed at building relationships, then we can create the best work environment possible.

A Healthy Office That Works

Anna's organization is like none I have ever come across in terms of its natural aptitude for using the Eight Steps. It is a large nonprofit operating in many states, but it has a small feel to it. Everyone works incredibly hard, busy all the time, but no one neglects their families or is asked to do so. There are plenty of phone calls during the day involving family, most everyone leaves by 5:30 P.M., and it's okay to occasionally duck out for a family crisis.

The easy integration, every day, of shared family problems and hard work guarantees a greater awareness in everyone that they are viewed as people above and beyond their capacity as workers. Everyone knows who is on the way to the dentist, who is limping and may need an operation, who has to go home on time to prepare supper tonight to lessen a spouse's burden, and who is going off to the gym because he's been devouring too many chips in the last few months. There is an integration of the personal and the professional in this office that does not make the day of work into either a waste of time or a group therapy session. These colleagues' identities as nonworkers are so clearly integrated into the workplace that it makes the actual work itself into a discreet task to be performed with as much skill as possible but as one of many components of an identity that others honor and respect. This artful combination seems to induce incredible productivity.

The organization is not a perfect family, of course. There are conflicts right beneath the surface, but they are subtle and seem to be successfully negotiated by introspection on the part of various workers. Most of the real conflicts are not personal but rather professional—how to solve the complex problems involved in designing cutting-edge educational programs, which is their business.

Anna is at the core of this positive and successful environment. She is curious about the world, and this curiosity is infectious and keeps the spirit of the organization ever young and vibrant. She takes everyone seriously, is warm and encouraging, and has clearly promoted to senior positions people with similar character. Anna's not perfect either though. She is a consummate worrier, and her mind goes in many directions at once. As a result, the atmosphere in the office is often frenetic. For an outsider this contributes to the charm of the place, but I imagine for workers it can become tiring.

Anna's organization, by virtue of its culture, is particularly good at helping employees deal with who they are as human beings as well as who they are as workers. Many more of us, however, mistakenly identify our value as human beings with our usefulness as workers. If we feel undervalued at work, we lose a positive sense of ourselves. In so doing we set the stage for struggles over prestige and power, because at rock bottom we do not value ourselves enough on an ongoing basis. No matter how fulfilling your job is or how much you enjoy your work environment, self-respect must exist independently of uncontrollable factors such as recessions, surpluses in the marketplace, changes in national regulations, bad managers, and so on.

Everyone deserves respect and appreciation when they put in an honest day's work. Every single day, however, tough, even brutal decisions are made by businesses to remain competitive, and Step One of the Eight Steps asks us to explore ahead of time how we are going to cope if we unexpectedly find ourselves unemployed. Business partners and employers also have to ask themselves how everyone can negotiate a work environment that abides by the tough standards of competition and hard work but that does not bury a worker's pride and sense of self. The atmosphere that Anna created in her organization generated in many people a positive sense of self that could withstand setbacks at work, but it is also true that she clearly gathered people who were already skilled at this most important task of self-care.

When I look for signs of health in an office, I look for what characteristics the coworkers have in common. Generally there is a kind of ripple effect, for both good and ill, in terms of who gravitates to and who stays in any given office. That means that the issue of character is profoundly important for determining the health and future of any organization.

Whether people value themselves is an essential component of any office. As workers we must find answers inside of us to profound questions about our basic value, and those answers must provide us with enough strength to withstand setbacks at work. How we are going to care for ourselves as human beings, beyond our capacity to work, is the essential question. Imagine tomorrow that we lost the use of our limbs, or that we were suddenly thirty years older. Who would we be in our own eyes? Would we fall apart, devastated? Surely we hope that children and adolescents do not fall apart because they cannot be as independent as adults. We expect and hope that their sense of self can cope with dependency. We must expect no less of ourselves as adults.

A good exercise is to imagine ourselves unable to work, and then to see and feel the love that parents or others have given us at one point or another in our lives. Imagining love that is directed at us unconditionally, without our present capabilities, can make us appreciate our work skills even more as special gifts that we have over and above our inherent worth as human beings. The goal here is to love ourselves. Everyone, from the wealthiest to the poorest, from the least educated to the most educated, has to face the limits of success, the limits of human accomplishment that time and age impress upon our existence. If we only think of ourselves as workers, we must come to a sense of bitter loss and failure at some point—unless we value more inside of us than work. That is a hard thing to do, but it is critical to preventing and healing our most profound work-related conflicts.

We can remember the very old whom we treasure, the very young whom we love, the fragile plants and animals that we have cared for, and imagine them inside of us. We can imagine all those vulnerable and precious beings, like beautiful children, as if they lay hidden beneath our armor of daily, combative usefulness. We can see them always waiting to emerge when we need to remember that we are not warriors deep down but simple, fragile beings temporarily on this earth.

Wounded Workers and Office Warriors

If we move from the example of Anna's organization to its opposite, a conflict-ridden office, we see people with similar needs but who fulfill those needs in a different, destructive way. Many people in such situations oppose or denigrate each other because they are trying, in a misguided way, to feel good about themselves. Wounded workers become office warriors in order to find meaning and worth, but it is a self-defeating enterprise. Whatever temporary gains there may be are offset by the injuries incurred by revenge attacks. Moreover, the harder a person works to become an office warrior, the more hopelessly delayed to older age will be issues of self-worth, when many buried regrets will spring to the surface.

It is hard not to engage in battle with office warriors when under attack. War is so contagious. In such situations, however, if we can manage to overcome our injuries long enough to acknowledge what we appreciate about others, it may be able to trigger reflection in them and a move away from self-defeating forms of combat.

In the professional environment it is particularly worthwhile to avoid conflict, because our workplaces involve their own rituals of communication and behavior and many things cannot be said and done without serious consequences. As we approach workplace conflicts through the Eight Steps, we must bear in mind that it may be harder than with family conflicts. Customs and rules of confidentiality may make it difficult to find an outsider, such as a member of the clergy or a mediator, to guide us through the conflict. It may not be possible, without being in a position of significant power, to bring a mediator into the workplace. More often than not we are on our own, without outside intervention. That is why the development of our character and skills becomes critical to keeping our work relationships healthy or to healing them as quickly and completely as possible when they are damaged.

Overcoming Poor Leadership

Donald was the forty-five-year-old CEO of a telecom company that was owned jointly by a group of experts in the field. He was fortunate to be in a position in which he supervised a team of employees; however, the company always seemed to be lurching from one crisis to another. Relatively minor controversies, such as who had the bigger office, who was taking vacation at a particular time of year, and how much everyone earned, turned his staff against one another, and no effort on his part seemed to diffuse the situation. His team simply could not work together. When Donald asked everyone repeatedly to cooperate, his plea fell on deaf ears.

I was fortunate to be an outside party to the corporation's conflict. I was friends with several of the partners and offered advice wherever I could. From that vantage point I could observe everyone's behavior. Right away I sensed the importance and centrality of the CEO in setting the stage for the problems. Everyone complained about him. He seemed somewhat erratic to me as well, alternatively friendly and caustic, rather unpredictable. That in itself can cause major leadership problems and help to create a conflicted culture.

So what was it about Donald that didn't sit right with his peers? I gathered from a variety of sources that he had a curious problem with truth telling. No matter how nice he appeared to be on the surface, he seemed to be holding a great deal of aggression inside that came out in the form of frequent lying. Lying was a way of solving intractable problems that he as the leader was supposed to solve in a more constructive manner. It also seemed to be a way to get even with everyone, by screwing around just a little bit with their brains and with the truth.

Donald hated any sort of open argument or conflict, and to prevent it from breaking out he would give in to his team members whenever they pressured him into giving bonuses, or bigger office space, or a special vacation. He would sometimes give in to two people at the same time, promising them the same thing, and then lie to get out of the bind!

I had no real access to Donald, but I did know and respect a number of the senior coworkers, all of whom co-owned the company. I reflected at length with them on the nature of the problems that they were facing. I explored with them the lessons of the first three steps: Be, Feel, and Understand. We started to realize that Donald was basically a good person who seemed unable to face tough conflicts head on, which got him and everyone else into trouble. We also explored how the deceptions and avoidance strategies brought out the worst in everyone else, and how their own character tendencies ended up feeding the problem.

In exploring the first three steps, they started to notice old issues in the corporation that had never really been resolved, and how Donald's character and their own flaws exacerbated the situation. Old unspoken resentments that may have been quietly forgotten or forgiven in a positive working environment marched to the fore due to the untrustworthy environment and its latent hostility. I call this phenomenon "cascading grievances," and it is a particular danger when leadership in any group has not faced basic questions about itself and its character (Be).

Based on my advice offered through my contacts with some of the partners, the co-owners started to engage the next two steps, Hear and See, which helped them push the corporation in a better direction. Unfortunately, they were unable to involve Donald in this process due to his strong resistance. He had serious problems with trust. The step of Imagine led to anticipation of what the corporation would look like under better management. The shareholders came to a place of understanding in which they honestly thought about Donald's interests as well. Donald still had a role to play in the company, they felt, but he was not satisfactory as the CEO. They came to the conclusion that Donald would be better off as a co-owner and team member rather than as the manager.

It is quite likely that if these co-owners had not taken

the bull by the horns and engaged in this process, their company could have easily been damaged, perhaps beyond repair. Corporations have fallen apart from far less pressure, especially in a highly competitive environment. These proactive co-owners saved the corporation, and the conflict was resolved in a way that was much better for them as well as for Donald in the long run.

It's too bad that Donald didn't allow himself to become more engaged in the process. He could have come to know himself better. He could have faced head-on his tendency to avoid conflict, weaned himself away from lying, and developed a healthier approach to conflict management and leadership. In a conflict, or even to avoid conflict, the more participants who engage the Eight Steps, the better off a work situation will be. At the same time, if it proves impossible to include everyone, the process will still yield benefits for each individual who engages the steps.

Discovering Meaning and Worth

Tom is a warm and loving person who has worked passionately his whole life in the nonprofit sector in order to make the world a safer place. He has spent much of his career with one organization dedicated to youth education. Tom gave up a career in business in order to do this work, and it has always troubled him because his accomplishments matter so much to his self-esteem. He was the child of working-class parents, and his professional accomplishments and intellectual abilities were a key antidote to the feelings of inferiority that he harbored.

Tom's troubles with his work evolved slowly, almost imperceptibly. He prides himself on being a critical thinker, and he started to have questions about the style and character of his organization. The organization had a good many flaws that were starting to get to Tom after many years. One thing that bothered him was that their stated goals focused on youth, and yet young people had become more and more excluded from the leadership of the organization. There were also subtle racial prejudices in play, or at least this is how it appeared to Tom. This bothered Tom because it so violated the purported aims of the organization, to transform the lives of all young people with better values. More importantly, the organization's prejudices called into question why Tom had given up a different life. The whole point of giving up a more lucrative and predictable career was to engage in an idealistic transformation of the world that focused on youth. But if the organization was tinged with prejudice and exclusion, then Tom had given up security and prestige for nothing, he felt. Others in the organization vigorously denied these charges and felt that the organization was evolving slowly, overcoming problems of the past, and that Tom was just too rash and angry.

Every long-standing group has a certain style to the way members interact and keep the peace. Tom's organization was no exception, and that's where Tom began running into trouble. He found himself violating more and more of the group's norms. He no longer felt capable of strictly adhering to the established rules of civility given the hypocrisy that he felt was present. But Tom got wrapped up in his own world of resentments, his own desire to right the wrongs of the organization. On one level this was good because maybe Tom's energy and criticism could shake things up a bit. On another level he was destroying good relationships and increasingly risking the leverage that he had in the organization by alienating numerous peers.

Was Tom alienating people because he was out of line in his criticisms, or was it because they did not want to face the issues he was raising? Was it a little bit of both? These are the kind of murky areas of conflict that can afflict a person's thoughts for months, even years, as he tries to disentangle what exactly is going on in reality. It takes understanding to work through these matters, but it takes much more. What we have learned is that we are creating and re-creating our realities all the time. Tom is creating his reality just as are the other members of the group. If we only try to understand, then we may never do anything about improving ourselves, our vision, our relationships. Understand is a critical step, but if that is all that is done then it is just a passive diversion.

I knew Tom from graduate school, and we spent some time talking about these issues. We analyzed his situation together, and we talked at great length about Understand. But it was Step One, Be, that unlocked many interesting issues for Tom. His struggles seemed to be with the basic question of his own legitimacy and value as a person. Out of too little confidence in himself he perhaps overidentified with the organization and took on their failings as his. So, when Tom struggles against problems in his organization, he is really struggling with himself on these same matters. He wonders, "Has my life been meaningful? Is my existence worthwhile, or am I just taking up space? Did I take the right or wrong path?"

Tom desperately wanted to make up for things the organization had failed to achieve. That is a noble sentiment, but it is also a prescription for great pain and endless conflict. At a certain point we need to acknowledge our inherent value as human beings, sacred beings, *independent* of what we can do, what we can change, or what we can repent of. That is not to say that a life of repentance is not a worthy goal, but we must love our lives independently of whether we achieve this goal, or independently of whether our identity rises to the achievement of something as elusive and ill-defined as repentance. Repentance can easily become a phantom goal that torments us with a permanent lack of completion. Often we must let go of conditional love and conditional hate of ourselves precisely in order to engage in profound change.

For his own good, on a personal and professional level, Tom needed to face some of his more combative characteristics. He had a tendency to beat up himself and others for imperfection, but by fighting such battles he was undermining the humanitarian goals for which he had worked so long and so hard.

Tom needed to hear and see his interactions at work

with a more dispassionate eye. Equally important, Tom had to dream of a better future; he had to create a vision of what he wanted the last third of his professional life to look like. This vision would give him the capacity to bring peace to his inner and his outer life as a professional. Finally, he had to forgive himself and others for failing to live up to ideal visions. Forgiveness is one of our hardest tasks, particularly the act of self-forgiveness.

Tom and I have continued to talk over time, and he is now in a place of much greater peace than he once was. This has also led him into renewed and better relations with most everyone at his workplace.

Partnering and Opportunities for Growth

Cooperation on business trips provides an interesting opportunity for discovering our strengths and weaknesses in working relationships. A trip away from the office is a time of discovery. When accompanied by a business partner, we often experience relationships in new and exciting ways, often striking up friendships.

There are also risks. Sleeplessness is common on trips, and therefore so is increased irritability. People are not as governed by ingrained inhibitions that may be typical of the office atmosphere, and some behaviors may emerge that are unexpected.

The predictable routine of office life generally evolves over time. In the context of that routine we achieve a certain amount of control and power over our lives. Everyone, even children, need to feel this sense of control. For example, I have noticed how important it is to my little daughter that she knows where her toys are at the beginning and ending of every day and to have just a little time with them. No matter what else happens on any given day, she has her favorite things that she can control in some way. People need the same thing in some measure in office environments, but trips can disrupt that sense of stability.

Offices often have domineering personalities, and domineering people tend to put the rest of us a little off balance. If we continue to work reasonably well with such people, then it is usually because we have achieved some unstated agreements on boundaries of control. If, on the other hand, I am the one that tends to be domineering, then it is likely—assuming my partnerships are relatively successful and happy—that I have learned my own limits with other workers. All these negotiated boundaries can change on work trips.

On a trip, or at a conference, I may become very controlling, out of anxiety or loss of inhibition. On the other hand, someone else may try to control me in ways that are completely unexpected. Suddenly many things have to be arduously negotiated, such as arrangements for transportation, food, or meetings. It is possible for all hell to break loose.

Under such circumstances, friction and conflict can occur between anyone, even those who are usually close friends. There are characteristics in a colleague that may shock you, and it may shake your confidence in how you chose your partners in the first place. Your colleague may drink too much; alcoholism may bring up strong feelings of anxiety or fear in you that you may not know what to do with. You may discover that your colleague treats waitresses or flight attendants badly, in a way that you never would have imagined. You may discover a reckless streak in your colleague that makes you feel unsafe, or that she is incredibly boring and you hadn't realized it before. You may discover that you are utterly incompatible in terms of dividing up power and control, but it never dawned on you before because circumstances didn't raise these issues.

On the positive side, you may deepen friendships and trust on trips because you have time to discuss things that would never come up at the office. You may discover that a colleague who you thought was a pain in the neck is dealing at home with a family tragedy and your attitude may shift from annoyance to admiration, or at least tolerance for his or her foibles. Many shifts in relations are possible.

We need to negotiate these moments well in order to make them work for better relations. The first and foremost step is self-awareness—what you're experiencing and how your actions are affecting the situation. The second and most important step is studying your colleagues, listening and watching their interactions, and learning. All of this should lead to the third group of steps, which involve communication and cooperation, in other words, Imagine, Do, and Speak.

Paying attention to all of the Eight Steps can transform business trips into opportunities for growth in workplace relationships. It is true that you may learn things that will make you more cautious about a colleague. This is an opportunity, however, because the more aware you are about both your own foibles and those of your colleagues, the more prepared you will be to handle conflict effectively and successfully should it arise between you.

Negotiating Personal Styles and Needs at Work

My own work trips with partners can be particularly intense, complicated, and even risky. Work to heal international conflicts can be particularly conflict-inducing! It puts stresses and strains on relations between the best of friends, especially because any misused words in public can sometimes bring the entire effort crashing down. The burden felt to solve serious conflicts where people are being hurt can become intense. There are also professional risks because there are profound emotions at work that, if unexamined, could compromise your effectiveness and your reputation. Many business professionals, entering a new situation, will present themselves publicly as a model of efficiency and cooperation. They have to—they are selling their own professionalism as well as their product, and so there is added pressure to prevent team conflict. If they end up fighting in front of clients, for example, they can look pretty silly.

I will never forget one time traveling with a small group

of people who represented a coalition of organizations who had put on a fabulous conference together about transforming relationships in the workplace. We were on a plane, on our way to receive an award for our work at the conference, and people were bickering the entire trip! I think it was about who would receive the award or what would be said. At the time I remember thinking to myself, "What is wrong with this picture?" Now I look back and I have to laugh at the absurdity of the moment.

Everyone, including professionals in conflict resolution, has personal issues that can occasionally drive them toward argumentative moments and general irritability. One colleague to whom I was particularly close, John, had precisely the opposite working style as me in almost every way. On trips, he plans everything, so he gets frustrated with meetings that were planned weeks in advance that don't work out. I do not care as much, feeling rather that if "they" didn't want to meet with me then it was never meant to be. I am much more interested in taking maximum advantage of new opportunities once I find myself in them. The more unpredictable the situation, the more comfortable I feel. I tend to focus too much on intellectual discussion and John tends to steer the conversation toward feelings. He wants to do everything together with me, and I am always longing on such trips for some solitude. He keeps to a schedule, thinking often about the next appointment. I focus on the eyes before me and am often ready to suspend other meetings and talk for six hours if my eyes have really connected with someone.

Few people seem to be able to match the amount of hours I am usually prepared to listen and talk, and it is not always practical, and I thank God that John is a schedule keeper.

John sleeps like a log, and, to put it nicely, lets everyone within a two-block radius know that he's asleep. I, on the other hand, can have an espresso on Tuesday and have trouble sleeping Wednesday night, and so sleeping in the same room with John is like something you'd see in a Laurel and Hardy skit. I remember one night, stuck in a hotel room together, we tried desperately to place our two mattresses at the farthest corners of the room, with my mattress ending up halfway into the bathroom. So you can see the prescription for some pretty endless bickering that we have done on trips. Oddly enough, we were the closest of friends before the trips, and we have remained so. The arguments have led to many discussions about our fears and problems, and it led to much growth in both of us.

Good friends tend to be especially effective at hearing and speaking to each other. That is true of John and me. If we have a problem, we can talk forever. Now, Peter is just about as different from John as you can imagine. He is extremely quiet, almost poker-faced. It's next to impossible to tell if he is elated or resentful. Many times I have found that kind of stoicism quite enjoyable, a relief from the emotion-laden encounters that I often have. Of course, it is a complicated affair when you are having meeting after meeting with your partner and third parties and you never know what your partner is thinking. Poker-faced is an understatement! It is true that Peter's reticence can sometimes drive me mad. On the other hand, it creates an interesting kind of drama, because I await anxiously at the end of the day for a series of verdicts on our encounters. I suppose I would not find it so enjoyable if I did not trust Peter's opinions.

Peter is insightful, incredibly experienced, patient, and wise. So when we partner there really has never been conflict—but there could have been. What we have done is condition ourselves to a great deal of self-awareness and observation, knowing our negotiables and our nonnegotiables, what we could compromise on and when we absolutely needed our own way.

Flexibility in Relations

Indeed, a basic part of preventing and healing business conflicts is training ourselves to adjust to each colleague's unique style. Quite often this induces our colleagues to make the same kind of adjustment to accommodate us. Too much accommodation, however, can be unhelpful as well. We must be conscious of creating a proper balance between accommodation and self-assertiveness.

Sally is a partner of mine who often errs on the side of being too agreeable, too much of a listener. She often tends not to let you know what she feels strongly about. This behavior too can set partnerships on the road to trouble, because resentment festers and comes out in the long run anyway. What I have done with Sally is, first of all, make many mistakes! I have often offered too many suggestions and too much advice, not realizing that I needed to resist the urge to advise and instead make space for her to speak and be heard. I also realized that Sally, like Peter, is a person of fewer words, with each word being significant. I come from a culture in which there is a proliferation of words and the full picture comes out by distillation of words. She comes from a culture of few words where the key to understanding is not distillation and summarization but rather deciphering, eliciting a great deal of insight from few words.

Steven is a work and travel partner who does not fit any of the previous examples. He is a man of fewer words than I tend to produce, but he can go on for quite a bit too! He can get pretty raunchy as well, unlike most of my other colleagues who tend to be obsessed with civility, sometimes to a fault. He is tough, even crass when he talks through complicated human problems, but he is extremely sensitive to other people's pain in many other ways. Steven is brilliant but emotional, and while he has strong opinions about what must happen in the future, and a certain kind of intellectual or visionary arrogance, he always quietly listens. He backs down before the strong opinions of others and gives them the space to express themselves without necessarily giving up his own views. Steven is a visionary, always bringing difficult conversations about tragic conflicts back to the art of the possible. He searches every articulation of a problem for what it can teach about solutions.

Steven is a mentor but also a friend, and, as with all colleagues, he is a competitor. Competition is part and parcel of work. It is when we pretend it is not that it ends up slapping us in the face. People can feel betrayed when they are led to believe that there is no competition and then suddenly it appears in the relationship. Competition can spur productivity and can go hand in hand with friendships and partnerships in the workplace. If, on the other hand, we emphasize it to the exclusion of all other values, then competition sucks the life out of us and our relationships. It is the subtle lessons of self-awareness, of Be, that teach us the art of balance on this front, and this makes us into good colleagues as well as healthy competitors.

Friendly Competition

There is really no way to escape the fact that every day at work you are called upon to perform, and to perform well. The best kind of colleague to have—and to be—at work is someone who knows himself well, who is eager to perform, and who is ambitious. There may be times that, in a spirit of playful or sportsmanlike competition, you and such a colleague will be contending for the same goal, either a prize or a bonus. This requires great attention to the lessons of self-awareness if the competition is to strengthen the work environment. It is also the case, however, that colleagues expect support or loyalty at the same time. That is where the other Eight Steps are so crucial. It is a subtle process of distinguishing between healthy competition and when you are actively undermining a relationship with others. Furthermore, conflicts erupting from competition are bound to happen, and therefore healing skills become crucial in overcoming the hurt that has been caused.

As an example, I can talk from experience about the unique culture of universities, in which there are often not many prizes to go around and the financial bonuses are almost silly. But the stock and trade of professors is wise insights and discoveries that no one else has achieved. Every day, in every meeting, there can be playful encounters of banter and competition; often I am overwhelmed by the brilliance of a colleague, and I have to admit, "She's really good!" If you have made peace with yourself by following through on the Eight Steps, then you should be able to celebrate this person's insight.

The Eight Steps are not meant to deny a healthy approach to ambition and accomplishment, but rather to negotiate and moderate this human need in such a way that it heals rather than injures, that it contributes to feelings of self-worth rather than feelings of humiliation and defeat, that it binds good colleagues together rather than tearing them apart. Competition is at the core of the business world, but it can either create a ruthless society both inside and outside the workplace or spur everyone on to achieve his or her highest potential. The choice is ours.

LOVE

The Eight Steps at Home

I counseled a couple who were contemplating getting married, Sarah and Joe. Joe was talkative and commanding in his style, but in an endearing way. He seemed so eager to make everything work out; he set up the appointments and was exuberant in his appreciation of me. Sarah, by contrast, was silent to such a degree that even the smallest amount of dialogue seemed painful for her. At first I thought it was with outsiders that Sarah had difficulty, but it started to dawn on me that Sarah was like this most of the time and especially when it came to any substantive conversation about relationships or the future with Joe. I tried to elicit as much as I could from her and listened patiently to Joe's rather lengthy attempts at compensation for Sarah's silences.

There was something endearing about this couple.

> LOVE: TO APPLY THE EIGHT STEPS TO EACH OF OUR DAY-TO-DAY FAMILY RELATIONSHIPS IN SUCH A WAY THAT PREVENTS CONFLICTS AND HEALS OLD ONES THAT PERSIST.

There was a gentleness about both of them that did not set off any alarm bells of physical or psychological abuse, and yet Sarah seemed unable to express her feelings on why she did or did not want to move toward marriage. The irony is that they came to me with a date for the marriage already in place, and the ostensible reason for seeking me out was for my services as a rabbi. Yet they were having trouble agreeing on what steps to take next, their long-range plans, and their living arrangements after the wedding.

I got nervous about the pressure of wedding plans when I sensed almost immediately that there were some basic issues that needed to be worked out separately and also between them as a couple. I asked them to experiment with conversations away from all pressure, in a pleasant context. I also asked Sarah to really look into her heart and think about what she wanted to communicate, and I asked Joe to work especially hard to be prepared to listen, to not jump in with help or advice. Joe's immediate instincts were to push hard at communication in such a way that could easily silence communication. Joe had a need to complete communication and bonding, and Sarah seemed to have a need to protect herself, to insulate herself from complete honesty.

Both of these folks were kind and gentle, yet it was not clear at all to me that Sarah really wanted all this. Her eyes said no, and yet her mouth said yes, as did some of her actions. It was as if she were not connected to her inner self, to her sense of her own being. She needed to start with Be and then move to the other steps, especially Speak and Do. Joe needed to discover the value of Hear, even if it meant hearing silence, because silence is a teacher also. Silence reveals as well as conceals, even though it can be deafening and painful.

In my work of healing conflicts I and my colleagues look for cultural differences that may explain the root of conflicts. The effects of culture can be quite subtle. Silence, for example, is particularly interesting because it is considered bad by some cultures and good by others. Silence can suggest hostility to some people but respect to others.

I wanted to be sure that in this case culture was not the defining reason for this couple's problems, and I did discover, in fact, that each one of them was conforming rather stereotypically to their different cultural backgrounds, Sarah coming from a rather stoic, New England rural background and Joe coming from an immigrant, urban background.

After a great deal of listening on my part, however, I came to the conclusion that this was not about culture. Sarah was fundamentally conflicted between a part of her that wanted to keep the relationship and part of her that wanted to hold on to her old living situation. She knew who she had been but not who she was willing and ready to be. It was never clear to me how much of this was mixed up with doubts Sarah had about Joe or whether the match was right. She was so silent that only she could know.

I heard some time later that they called off the wedding, and I was saddened but also relieved. I met Joe a couple of years later and he was happily married to someone else, but I never knew what happened to Sarah. I sensed that Joe had been too pushy about plans, but, in the end, he understood his needs and he decided to move on, as painful as that was. I sensed that both had looked into themselves and that this exploration had led them to the unhappiness of breaking up marriage plans but to a better life path that in the long run would make them happier. Our best-laid plans can go awry sometimes, but above all we need to be honest in our relationships. This couple had to work on several of the Eight Steps in order to carefully consider their family life together and its consequences. In this case it led to separate lives, but an unexamined, unhappy life together would have led to far more misery down the road, especially for Joe's ten-year-old daughter.

Constant Attention

Family relationships need to be founded upon a web of solid emotional commitments, for this web is the lifeblood of our lives. Conflict is part and parcel of family life, and yet there must be a foundational commitment that transcends conflict, and this has to be built constantly.

At home, in our families, conflict will involve personal issues and needs, needs that are felt at a more raw level, really at the core of our being, and this is why Step One, Be, is so indispensable to the Eight Steps. Issues of competence and competition at the workplace may trigger the strongest emotions in some people, but for most people it is family and love relationships that affect them most.

All relationships require regular nurturing; leaving them unattended is risky. We tend to be especially neglectful with family relations because we assume that they will always be there, but this is an illusion. Children grow up and move away, parents grow old and die, and siblings can live forever on angry terms. A sibling can be a lifelong friend, or someone who you see, uncomfortably, only at family celebrations and tragedies—as long as parents are alive—and then finally to pay your respects. What a waste of an opportunity for a wonderful relationship.

The glue that keeps families together is not cement because it can be and often is loosened and lost. That is why we need to engage our relatives in reflection and healing on a regular basis, so that whatever time we have on this earth with our blood relations becomes immortalized in some way, a permanent monument to the value and dignity of our family, something that can weather the precarious impact of time and mortality.

Engaging family through an awareness of the Eight Steps is a powerful process because it offers so much possibility for lasting fulfillment. Whereas a work crisis may have to be handled quickly, most family relations and family conflicts evolve over time, reach crisis moments, and then revert back to a steady drone of uncertainty. This provides room for two things: experimentation and the healing effects of time for reflection and growth. Both of these things can lead to long-term growth if we see our relationships as part of a lifetime odyssey.

As long as we do not become complacent and stuck, we have a great deal of maneuvering room to work on our inner lives and outer family relationships. Most importantly, family life often involves key transitional moments, such as births, new members, deaths, and illnesses that, if experienced with wisdom, become opportunities to move ourselves and fellow family members in new directions. This is where a consciousness of the Eight Steps and their basic messages prove to be so useful.

Rebuilding What Is Broken

One of the most important challenges facing us is how to cope with broken family situations and recover the capacity to heal and rebuild relationships. A man, we will call him Sam, moved along in his marriage thinking that everything was basically working out. He had never gotten along with his wife's mother, and in fact there was always something strange about the family that he had never quite understood, such as a passion for secretive gestures and arrangements.

When I met up with Sam at one of the universities I was attending, he came to me with a startling revelation. He had found out quite by accident that when his wife was going home to her family in Mexico she was also going home to another husband. I almost fell to the floor when I first heard this.

As I sat listening to Sam, I asked myself, "What kind of process did this fellow need in order to deal with this potentially catastrophic situation?" Because there were no children involved, it was a straightforward question of whether he would continue any relationship with his wife, and he decided on his own that it was inconceivable, even if she did change or want to come back to him. Sam had to cope with what had happened in this relationship. He was deceived, plain and simple, but in order to move on and try as best as he could to make sure that this experience did not damage future relationships, he needed to assess his role in the marriage. He needed to look inside himself and distinguish between what he wanted to change in himself and what there was about him that was absolutely good and blameless.

It is absolutely natural and normal for someone who has been deceived and victimized to wonder, "What's wrong with me? How could I have been so naïve?" Even as it is critical that we don't take the blame for all the problems in a relationship, self-examination is an opportunity for us to grow and evolve into someone who will be happier, wiser, and better protected from future catastrophe.

It turns out that Sam's wife's family was a part of the deception from the beginning of the relationship. They had some pretty strange and dysfunctional approaches to furthering their own needs. Their particularly virulent strand of selfishness saw marriage purely as an act of material gain. A sad reality, but it was not up to Sam to heal them or change them. If Sam had had children with his wife, then this would have required him to engage the other Eight Steps in order to cope with sharing the children while causing a minimum of damage to them. But in this case Sam's main task was to recover, to heal himself, and to grow as a person so that he could look back on this terrible episode and see that what he had learned could lead him to greater happiness in the long run.

I was able to help Sam examine the inevitable consequences of life lived as a lie. One day, one way or another, this bizarre set of lies was destined to ruin his life, at least temporarily. That it came out when it did allowed him to recover, move on, and create a new life. I was also able to offer Sam critical spiritual support that affirmed his value as a person. People who have been injured radically by others, who have been treated as an object to be used by those they trusted the most, tend to feel a loss of worth. Whenever we know that this has happened to us it is critical to seek out other trusting relationships, such as with a teacher or pastor who has a good reputation. We need to be in a position to have others affirm our value. Of course, most of this affirmation needs to come from inside of us, but Sam did something healthy by reaching out to others.

Be, as a step, is not about going it alone but rather about knowing ourselves well enough and valuing ourselves enough to then reach out for help, even while considering how to reach out and help others. Sometimes we need others whom we respect or trust to remind us that, despite those who have injured us, life in a relationship is better than solitude; it is the essence of human fulfillment even when sometimes it invites victimization. Our search for happiness will push us right back into relationships. Intuitively, Sam entered into a relationship with me and with others, which strengthened his own internal process of change.

Months later Sam came to me with some conflicts that erupted in his workplace, and we had some good discussions about his interactions as a manager and coworker. There too he had to do some important self-examination that led to practices involving the Eight Steps. I was proud of him—he had secured his basic sense of self from the ruinous place in which he had found himself. As difficult as the workplace conflicts were, they paled in comparison to the family onslaught he had suffered, but all indications were that he was on the road to recovery.

Growth and Transformation

Sam's case and the case of Sarah and Joe reveal some hard realities about family life and conflict. In fact, I hardly meet anyone in my work who does not seem to be recovering from pain in childhood due to family problems. At the same time, if you read many biographies you know that some of the most accomplished people in the world have had what they describe as a terrible childhood.

It is strange that some people emerge from terrible family situations empowered to do extraordinary things in the world. Some of them never forgive their parents, despite their own accomplishments and success, whereas others do reconcile. Some people never recover, never grow personally or professionally, and can never get over bad or abusive relations in the past. In all these cases there is pain. Then there are those who never address the challenges in their family relations; there may be less conflict, less pain, but there is also no growth.

Growth is the operative word here. We all have heard the expression *growing pains,* but let's analyze it more from the point of view of conflict. Growth is change, and change means conflict between what was and what is about to be, between who I was (or who we were as a family) and who I am (or we are) about to become. To an extent, the pain associated with change is critical for the stability of both individuals and communities. If there were no painful boundaries between who we are and who we might become, then the slightest pressure or disappointment would lead us to be changing partners all the time, hurting our parents, children, and loved ones, and walking out of friendships and partnerships on a regular basis. This unsettled state of being is more about moving away from responsibility than it is about embracing growth.

But while seeking out drastic change for its own sake isn't something I'd recommend, the world is constantly forcing our bodies and minds to respond to changing circumstances in our own lives as well as in the lives of those we depend on. In ever so subtle ways we are always experiencing some death and rebirth, and therefore we must be feeling, in some corner of our beings, all the terror that an infant feels arising from the loss of the womb, of what was certain and safe.

I will never forget the moment I first looked into my eldest child's wide eyes. She had just come out of the womb and within seconds the nurses put her straight up to my face and had me cut the umbilical chord. But before I could even cut—and I was so dazed that they had to direct my arm— she looked straight at me. At that moment I think we both had the same terrified look on our faces. I, too, was experiencing a sort of birth, the birth of responsibility for another life, something I had avoided for a long time. I left behind on that day the status quo of my previous life as a life only for myself and the comfort of knowing that if I screwed up I screwed up for myself only. The interdependence of my wife and I was utterly different from then on, as the new reality of our child's absolute dependence upon us for food, protection, happiness, intellectual growth, and the rest sunk in. To be honest, I still can hardly fathom the extent of the responsibility. The pleasure and personal fulfillment of fatherhood— my birth as a happy father—would come, but even as I look back now, the terror of my rebirth is real to me to this day, and I do not feel the need to sugarcoat it. I know and my daughter knows how devoted I am to her.

Anyone who's done it knows that child rearing is hardly a comfortable or perfect process, but it is noble, even heroic. Most important to realize is that the pain of birth and growth is not just something that our children go through, it is something we adults go through as well, constantly. Yes, it causes many conflicts, internally and externally. But with practice, what we learn from the Eight Steps is that this perpetual state of birth and growth can yield happiness and contentment.

From Worry to Healing

I don't know anything on earth that is as powerful as the bonds of love that most parents have for their children. We all know the exceptions, and the media tends to sensationalize the worst examples of parental behavior. Most of us are not like that, however; on the contrary, if we make our children miserable it is often because we love them so much and, in our zeal, we tend to overreact to anything that endangers them. That includes our efforts to control them and protect them from the many ways in which they can and do hurt themselves or their future.

I remember when a friend's son got angry and kicked out a window in the family car. He had had temper tantrums before, but this kind of destruction just astonished the father. At that moment my friend saw his son in a new way, and it left him speechless. He did not know how to begin to address the issue. I counseled him to remember that one of the shocks of growing up is the amount of power that we begin to possess. Children are constantly surprised by their own power. They may be acting as they have in the past, even playfully, but they now cause destruction. It shocks them but entices them as well, as all newfound power entices human beings. I listened carefully to the story, and I know this family well, and my sense was that there was nothing to be overly concerned about here. Certainly such behavior isn't to be condoned, but understanding the background and possible motivations of a conflict can help parents avoid overreacting and possibly provoking further and deeper conflict.

As calm as I generally am when engaging others on conflict, still I was somewhat unsettled by my brush with rage in my own children. My oldest daughter went through a difficult episode when she was six. She had gotten sick and had to stay home from school, and when she got better she resisted going back to school and started complaining about everything. We had intense fights around bedtime in particular, but the true horror came in the form of her mood swings—one moment she could be playful but then the slightest thing could send her into a rage. She would throw things and scream, saying terrible things when we called her to task for her behavior.

We had had conflicts before but we always worked them through. Suddenly, within a span of just a few weeks, I found myself needing to physically restrain her. It was a nightmare, and I remember glaring at her one time and just screaming, "You cannot treat us this way!" The desperation sneaked up on us like a thief. How could this have happened? What was going on? I started to realize that her rages triggered old things in me, old habits of reacting to rage in others. I was mortified when I realized that I was not in control of myself at these moments.

Finally we found out that her problems were physical, that she had terrible pain in her head, neck, and back that were responsible for changing her behavior. She had a mysterious, mononucleosis-like virus that would just not go away, causing her extreme pain and bad allergies on top of it. While we were insisting that our daughter should get ready for school, what she really needed was to sleep and heal. We thought she had entered into an adolescent-type state of rebellion, and we reacted against that, but what she really needed was great affection and massages to her back and head. I still feel the regret now as I write this, so long after the events.

After we realized what was going on and shifted completely our treatment of her, she calmed down remarkably, though the remnants of the illness and the dependency that it generated in her character remained for a long time, and this caused some tension. She felt doubly hurt, first by the illness in ways that she could not convey as a child, and then by us for the way we responded to her. This realization I held in my mind as I soothed her head and neck. I tried to make up for the past. We breathed in and out together, in the quiet of the night, as she lay down to sleep, and I helped her relax and deal with the pain. I was dealing also with my pain, and healing myself at the same time.

We had to learn in those months how to balance great gentleness for her in her recovery and, at the same time, recognize when she needed discipline to get back into a routine that would be healthy for her mental and physical states. It was a balancing act that required great sensitivity and some experimentation, as does good parenting in so many instances. We never completely knew when she was authentically exhausted and when we needed to step up the discipline. There were many unknowns that made our efforts necessarily imperfect. Working hard at the relationship and, at the same time, accepting the imperfections of one's efforts is one of the key challenges in all human relationships, and we knew that we were not always successful.

To my mind, the most important thing we did to nurture the relationship with our precious daughter was endless talking and listening to her, lots of apologies, and, above all, engaging the step of Understand. We were doing this to heal our relationship with her as well as to get her healthy. What is so extraordinary about children is how prepared, even eager, they are, at young ages, to forgive their parents. The Dalai Lama of Tibet often writes about those with whom he is in conflict being his most important teachers. How true it is.

Emulating What Is Positive in Those We Love

Another key in connecting with children is to allow the natural love of children for parents and parents for children to act as a guidepost of what to do even in the worst of situations. Parents must become the most important models of empathy, love, and forgiveness, which are the critical emotions that help heal conflicts. The older that children become, however, the more their ability to empathize and forgive becomes constrained by their need to establish an identity separate from their parents; they develop a natural resistance to simple emulation of their parents. This vital process in human growth and maturation can cause problems if we hold onto our anger and disappointment with flawed parents and, instead of moving forward with our lifelong quest for positive identity formation, fixate on the negatives of our parents. This is part of a larger phenomenon that is well known in human conflict, the tendency to define one-self against others, something examined excellently by Dr. Vamik Volkan in writings such as *The Need to Have Enemies and Allies*. Negative identity, built on the rejection of others, is a cheap way to establish identity. We find what and who we hate and then we define ourselves against them.

Unfortunately, it is possible to survive quite well on negative identity. Whole civilizations, at one point or an-other, build themselves up on hatred and demonization of someone else. But this course is superficial, inauthentic, and inevitably leads to misery and self-destruction. Even if it does not lead to personal misery in the short term, it almost al-ways generates a more miserable world.

A negative rejection of parents' identities by adoles-cents—or, indeed, adults—may be necessary temporarily for growth, but if we don't grow past that we end up as un-happy people stuck in adolescent rebellion for the rest of our lives. We tend to live inside anger, first as adolescents and then as adults, falsely assuming we have left adolescence simply because we have grown older. True personal growth, however, involves internalizing the lessons learned in the Eight Steps.

Negative identity is a miserable way to live, always focused on what you are not to the extent that it's all you think about. It's a trap. If, on the other hand, you build a positive sense of who you are, then you can feel close to parents who you know are flawed and not confuse them with your own identity. Such a positive approach sets the stage for continuing to develop a positive identity later on in life, as we graft onto ourselves that part of our parents' character that we have come to honor and appreciate.

The step of Feel is critical here in order that our positive feelings of love for our parents not get confused with our own search for Be. Feel is successfully negotiated to the degree to which Be, in a positive sense, is intact. That way positive feelings about our parents only strengthen our sense of self, whereas negative feelings about or assessments of our parents do not as easily overwhelm and destroy what we have achieved for ourselves in Be.

In some sense anger in children is the most fundamental test of Be, both for them and for their parents. It brings all the issues of life, conflict, and happiness into sharp relief. None of the stages of healing conflict can be successfully negotiated without a sense of positive identity being established in both parents and children. Clearly, when it comes to parents and children, the basic family unit, a successful engagement with Be sets the stage for the whole regimen of the Eight Steps.

The Fantasy of Perfection

Often we think of *perfection* as a positive word. It seems related to our aesthetic sense of beauty and our experience of pleasure; we talk of a perfect day, a perfect body, a perfect meal. But the truth is that fantasies of perfection plague human life in many ways. We develop unrealistic expectations of ourselves, of others, of our communities, or of our environment. The aspiration for perfection might stem originally from a healthy desire to improve ourselves or to improve the world, but obsession with perfection is destructive and must be confronted openly, especially as it applies to family relations.

At the heart of all addictions to perfection is a learned sense of ingratitude for what is, for what one has been given. That is why a daily regimen of prayer or meditation that focuses our minds on what we have been blessed with is utilized by millions of people as a powerful antidote to this self-induced misery. Why this comes upon us at certain points in life is an excellent subject of reflection for Step One of our work. Gratitude can be learned, and the tyranny of unsatisfied needs for perfection can be undone.

In the case of family, if we live day to day with some notion inside our heads of the perfect child or the perfect parent, it sets in motion a subtle form of family destruction. We pass on these messages in ever so subtle ways to young children and then we wonder why they complain so much about every little thing that does not go their way or every pain that they experience. We often teach them unknowingly to be dissatisfied, to expect perfect parents, to expect a day without challenges and a life without disappointment. If one person hurts us we may forget the dozen people who were kind.

What really is this thing called perfection? In many ways it is the opposite of life. Life is not perfect. Perfect bodies or perfect minds never grow, never age, never change. Perfect parents or children never fail, and they never say they are sorry because they have never done anything wrong. Perfection of this kind is like a beautiful Michelangelo statue, permanent, even an object of veneration, and useless in human relations. Ultimately this kind of perfection is dead, or an illusion, and it has no relationship to mortal lives, which are experienced vibrantly with all of their outrageous imperfections.

Our extended families grow and change by definition because we all get older. Families are filled with unknowns, experiments, mistakes, and learned improvements.

Marc Ross, a wonderful analyst of human conflict, cites interesting recent work on the idea of being "good enough" as opposed to being perfect. Marc cites the provocative idea that our ideal goal is to be "good enough." The "perfect" mother, the mother who fulfills every single need of her children, the mother who is always there, who always sacrifices herself for her children, is ironically imperfect because she is not giving her child the chance to become self-reliant. Self-reliance, a key goal of child rearing and maturation, requires imperfection in caregivers. I would add that the perfect mother is not providing a reasonable role model of how to live and balance one's own needs with those of others. That means that disappointment and the imperfect satisfaction of our needs by parents is a key to normal maturation. Imperfect parents give us the chance to strive, to change and improve ourselves, and to search for our own ideals and aspirations.

The celebration of imperfect parenting could be utilized as an excuse to ignore children's needs for attention, and that is not the intention. Everything is about balance, especially balance of everyone's needs in a family, but what we should focus on right now is the importance of imperfection in normal human development. Our own imperfections, and the imperfections of those we love, need to coalesce with the commitment to love and be grateful for one another, despite the imperfections and disappointments. The reality of imperfection requires the skill or moral quality of gratitude to produce the happiness we deserve in family.

One way that this hard lesson is learned by some people is when they themselves become parents. For this reason, I believe that everyone should care for children for a certain period of their lives, their own or someone else's. Whether this comes about through traditional or untraditional ways of parenting, the experience reveals secrets of life that are not found elsewhere. Children thrive on many adults giving them some attention, and adults can grow in surprising ways through responsible and loving interaction with children.

It is useful to say to ourselves, "Be grateful for what you have and the good that you did experience in childhood," and to reflect and meditate on that every day as a way to evolve into a state of contentment with our lives. By contrast, we can also reflect on the insidious demands of perfection and train ourselves to avoid the pitfalls of the fantasies of perfection. The inner world of family is an unpredictable odyssey, however, and sudden conflicts often will take us straight back to bitter disappointments of the past, no matter how much we have tried to train ourselves otherwise.

The past is always assaulting the present, and we cannot escape the challenge of family disappointments that live on in the present. How then will we cope with disappointment, imperfection, visions of what was lost in the past, and what we long for in the present? How do we confront the tyranny of thoughts of imperfection and feelings of ingratitude and distinguish that from what we can and should expect from family relations? The most important premise of the Eight Steps is focusing on who we want to become and on what we ourselves can do to improve our relationships because so many dynamics of conflict depend upon initiative, on who will persist in initiating healing relations. This is where individual initiative and experimentation, sometimes over the course of a lifetime, become crucial to confronting the ups and downs of lifelong relationships.

The Healing Road Home

I want to illustrate how the Eight Steps work in regard to the family by returning now to an exploration of my father, who died a few years ago after many years of illness. My father was simple in some ways and exceedingly complex in others. A man who many thought of as jolly and positive in his orientation, he was also plagued by feelings of self-doubt stemming from his relationship to his parents. I am convinced that he had a reading disability, which led to a profound sense of humiliation, especially because it was never outwardly acknowledged and dealt with constructively. In fact, I never saw him reading a book, except during a couple of years in midlife when he made a brave and successful attempt to pass the tests to become a real estate broker. In his youth he found solace not in books but in his looks, in his physique, and in his popularity with fast crowds, despite his intensely religious upbringing.

Based on conversations that I had with family members it was apparent that my father never received the love he craved from his earliest years and sometimes received insults and abuse from his own father. He grew into a man who hid his rage behind a mask of stoic toughness, a pliant, friendly attitude to customers in his own business, and a broad smile. He was one of the least understood people I have ever come across. He began his life as one of many children of an immigrant family and seems to have never gotten enough of the admiration he needed, at least not in comparison to his older brothers. At the same time he received a substantial amount of ridicule from his own father.

Dad did expose his rage at home in the early years of our family, and for more than one sibling it was rather hellish. I was spared the worst of those years because things began to calm down by the time I, the youngest by far, moved into my school years and into a greater awareness of the family dynamics. I was not a victim, but I witnessed a great deal early. I witnessed too much, and witnessing forges its own path to and out of hell. It carries its own kind of damage that can stay with you for the rest of your life.

As I grew older I disagreed with my father on many important issues and shared no interests with him, although we both spent a great deal of time together in the synagogue. His silence at all the important events of my young life was deafening, never a word of advice. Was it apathy, underconfidence, ambivalence about family roles? It's hard to say, but the impact was strong.

The family life my father created, far different from his public image, was the source of great conflict in those early years, the time of greatest family challenges when children are young and demanding. When he came home from World War II, the confrontations became brutal in the family, everyone used the weapons available to them—the ones, that is, that are designed to do the most damage. This just confirmed for my father everything he had felt since childhood, that no one ever showed him any respect and that perhaps he was not worthy of any. Respect is what he craved more than anything else in the world, for he often displayed excessive admiration for "heroic" men, including his father, who commanded respect and admiration from everyone. This was at the core of his interest in movies starring men like John

Wayne, Clint Eastwood, Gregory Peck, and George C. Scott. He desperately needed a fantasy life where everyone respected him.

Dad did have places in his working-class world where he received respect, places such as the doughnut shop and the barbershop in his native working-class town of Chelsea, Massachusetts. We were amazed to discover, after he died, how many people admired him. He did not need to conquer the world, but he did need a small oasis of honor, as most men do.

Dad was painfully aware, however, that respect gained in small, humble places, in poor, lower-class environments, would never be enough to win his elders' respect, his family's respect, his religious community's respect. In that world, wealthy business magnates, doctors, and professors reigned supreme on the respect scale, more with every passing decade of Dad's life. His was the changing world of second- and third-generation immigrants and their evolving attitudes toward status and success. In a certain way the forces of history ran right over his accomplishments, as it has for millions of working-class folks and World War II veterans.

I reached adolescence just about when Dad was getting older, much heavier, and sick. I watched this unfold through precocious, tormented eyes and with a mixture of fear, disbelief, and regret over what all this did to him. He seemed to get so little of what he needed emotionally in those years that food became an important refuge. I resented him, I feared him, and I developed an irresistible and radical compassion for him, all at once.

All was not bad, and in fact there are many good memories. Dad did have many healthy habits, he slept more soundly than any of us, and he had an incredibly strong emotional bond with his siblings, something that his parents had clearly done right in engendering. But he never seemed completely comfortable at home. He did not do the typical puttering around that middle-aged men do in homes that they have acquired through hard work. He craved work time outside the house, seven days a week, without exaggeration, and it is doubtful that he had to do all this work to make a living. Even Saturday nights he would return sometimes to work for a short time to check over properties he owned. Sunday he came home a little early, in the afternoon, then ate, watched television, and slept.

Home in those years was the place of the least success in his life, where he always felt a little ill at ease. He did not speak much to us children in those early years, and he seemed constitutionally incapable of offering spoken advice at even the most crucial junctures that his children faced in their years of growth. In general his family was long on small banter and short on heart-to-heart, well-articulated communication, whereas we children took refuge in long, endless conversations with Mom. All of this would change later, but in the early years of the family, and in Dad's middle age, our family interactions were baffling.

And yet I know that Dad loved me, and he showed it in many demonstrative but nonverbal ways, especially as he got old and sick. In fact, in the later years his relationships with all or most of the children improved. As the years went by I started to feel for him a mixture of sympathy, old fear, and growing affection, almost despite myself.

I spent years wrapped up in anger over what I could not get from my father. I could not get simple verbal communication about anything substantive. I could not get advice at critical junctures where I had made huge mistakes with my life, and I never could develop a sense of safety that my father would not lose his temper and become violent, as laughable as that prospect became with each new infirmity of old age. Time and age, though, never completely remove the terror of old violence, at least not for children with strong memories. I waited in vain for some honest apologies, to me and to others in the family, but such verbal gestures would never come.

Slowly it dawned on me that my father's body was deteriorating, that my mourning over what I never had from father would slip before long into mourning for everything I did not experience of parents when I had the chance. Mourning over death, present or future, has a way of putting all other forms of mourning into perspective.

As a boy, I hated television and fattening foods, but I often felt strangely compelled to watch television and eat those foods because Dad enjoyed them—and I still do! I was so saddened watching my father do this to himself, feeling that he was in denial about the way in which those addictions were killing him a little more every day. The doctors seemed to think so, but most gave up on trying to induce lifestyle changes.

As I became an adult I had to begin struggling with some basic Be questions. What is it that drives us to do exactly as our parents do and then resent them for it? Why and when do we emulate the worst in them rather than the best? Why did I spend those years mourning what Dad was not instead of appreciating who and what he was?

Many of us will dwell on our parent's failures and then, in a paradoxical move of bonding, make their failures our own. This is a typical but destructive way in which families bond. The compulsion for love and attachment is irresistible, but how we bond, with positive love or ambivalent love mixed with resentment, depends completely on us, and that is a hard thing to accept.

I was learning in those years the dangers of stereotype, especially liberal stereotypes of macho men like my father who are always much more complex than they appear. I started to realize that his fascination with tough men had little to do with his own instincts for war. In fact, he had avoided fighting during the war, and he seemed to go out of his way to avoid fighting and prejudice at work, even in a tough urban environment.

Once, a couple of months before he died, Dad looked

up at me, from the depths of a body contorted by stroke, and said, "I'm afraid." Simple, shared indulgences merged seamlessly in those last days with time spent together on assisted walks outside, the best walks of my life. Singing birds, trees, and ever darkening blue skies toward evening went hand in hand with a row of old brown telephone poles, which Dad leaned on for dear life, one at a time, each one reached after brave struggle, marking the short trail of his last heroic walks and his noble determination to hold on to his dignity.

These belated bonds seemed to make up for a lifetime of silence—the saddest time for the father, facing the steady loss of his vitality, and the most fulfilling moments of the son's life. Leaning on a telephone pole, choking up with emotion, he would say about his legs, "They're no good, they won't go," and I would be silent until he began to walk again. Leaning on the next pole, he would say, "I can't go on," and I would say, "You always do." Sometimes he would ask, "Why are you so good to me?" and I would be silent, and at other times he would ask again and I would say, "Because you deserve it," and then we would be silent, and the silence was as good as the words.

Dad died being loved and respected for his extraordinary physical and emotional perseverance, his good humor, and his generosity. He was even sought after by young nephews for advice—yes, advice. This last bit of appreciation, of him as advisor, confounded Dad as much as it confounded his family. Strange endings for a man embroiled in lifelong conflicts and silences with his immediate family.

Healing Step by Step

How can we make sense of this story from the point of view of the Eight Steps of healing conflicts? The Steps are a reservoir of information and potential healing that need to be adjusted to each and every situation. Some steps may become central and others peripheral depending upon what needs to be done but also what can be done in each relationship. It is also true that analysis of family problems requires a hard look at each situation in all its complexity and then a singular assessment of what is to be done. We have taken one example and looked at some of its complexity. Let's now go through the story with the Eight Steps specifically in mind and see what was done right.

Perhaps the main challenge in our family relationships is that my father had to face some hard issues about his past behavior, but he seemed constitutionally incapable of discussing this in an open way with anyone, least of all his children. In other words, the path of Speak was not easily open to him. On the other hand, much was going on inside of Dad in his later years, and these reflections, as a part of Be, led him to change in many ways. He seemed to do more active listening as he got older; I certainly sensed it in my relationship with him. He started asking questions and expressing curiosity about our lives, especially when he heard from my mother that something was wrong or not going well. He had a strategy of asking innocent questions that were pretty transparent, actually, in terms of what he was advising, but also quite endearing. I remember noticing in wonder how long and intently he listened to my sisters when they called long distance. In fact, once confined to the house after the stroke, he developed an amusing habit of not hanging up the phone and instead listening to all of the conversation, even when we were calling Mom. It did not feel like an invasion but like care.

The challenge when someone takes that long to evolve is that other family members, habituated to the old person, find it hard to actually accept new steps that a family member is taking. In hindsight I realize that Dad was really struggling with the steps of Be, Hear, and Understand for many years, decades even, before he actually broke through to build new habits and skills. These led him directly to a profound evolution in Do. He had always been good at symbolic gestures of care, but this became a predominant theme of his relations. It led to reciprocation, and it positively affected talking and listening as well.

I began to realize rather late that my father had been trying to communicate through Do for years and no one was really hearing him. From his cooking and his gifts to his affection, and his active expressions of pride in his children that he voiced to friends, he was sending a message, a message of reconciliation, a message of regret, of love. He was trying to communicate in many ways, and that, not words, is the most important building block of healing conflicts.

No one can fundamentally change his or her personality, but experience suggests that we are all capable of small shifts that are often surprisingly sufficient to heal wounds garnered over the lifetime of a troubled relationship. Sometimes it feels as if longstanding, troubled love relationships have a life of their own and that they are starving for, and ready for, even the smallest shifts that provide new life to the relationship. There is a reservoir of yearned-for love that is embedded in family ties, and that reality makes small shifts and gestures into big ones.

In the case of my family, even small changes in the habits of the father and the children, little indulgences in human foibles and a growing tolerance for small annoyances, seemed to set the stage for moments of reconciliation. It is amazing how easily family imperfections can be the symbol of impossible rifts and the pretext for "cosmic" battles in one decade and then in another decade be the subject of mild annoyance or even exuberant laughter. There is an extraordinary resilience of the human spirit always at work, and there is a resilience of the spirit of a family. We have but to stimulate it or discover it by virtue of the steps we take toward healing.

Small increments, small steps are the key. I even believe that after his stroke, in his own way, Dad began to bring out the best in his own siblings. Their bonds and joy with each other seemed to flower in a way that I had not seen in many years, all in the context of their visits to him when he was so impaired. One brother sat for hours during the day watching television with him. This newfound engagement with Feel paved the way for many subtle changes, including steps forward with Imagine on the part of those witnessing these changes, growth in one person setting in motion growth in others.

I remember now that several of us bought tapes for Dad because we knew how much he loved music. Once I put on a Nat King Cole tape and brought my mother into my father's bedroom, a room that really became the central social gathering place of the house. I had them dance together, and they really enjoyed the moment. Of course I knew how immobile and sick Dad was, and I knew there was a risk that the dancing might be awkward, even embarrassing if it should fail, but I also knew that dancing was something my parents relished together over half a century ago. I remember my niece was visiting at the time and I still can see her enormous smile, because I am not sure she had ever seen her grandparents dance together. This act introduced spontaneity into the situation, an indulgence in the joy of life at the present moment no matter what was coming.

I stood on the side of the bedroom the day of that dance as if I had completed a mission, a mission to bring a small bit of happiness into a hard struggle with disease. I watched quietly, with a sense of assurance that orchestrating that moment was my destiny and that nothing else in the world mattered—a hard happiness to accept for someone like me, obsessed with the world's troubles. I did nothing on that day that my siblings did not do before me, each trying in those years to use their imaginations to make my parents' lives a little bit better, to give well-deserved comfort to an imperfect father who nevertheless deserved all of our love and gratitude in his last years.

Many things about family relations will forever be consigned to the realm of mystery, but, as for myself, I do know that I could not have arrived at that audacious moment of Imagine if I had not spent years engaged with Be, Feel, Hear, Speak, Do, all the other Eight Steps. That is why the moment is seared into my memory as if it were the culmination of a journey, as if it were a reward for hard work. It was: It was part of my journey of healing.

HARMONIZE

The Eight Steps in the Community

I have had many wonderful students over the years who I have trained in conflict resolution. One student, Sam, whom I consider a colleague and a teacher in his own right, is a courageous religious peacemaker from Africa, a survivor of the Liberian war. Sam barely escaped with his life many times during that terrible genocide. He continues to put himself at risk in order to care for the victims of war across West Africa, organizing peacemaking activities and reconstruction in several countries. He has been formally trained in conflict resolution and yet far and away his greatest asset is his own character, his being. What is so remarkable about him is how he has recovered from enormous violence and transformed himself into a healer.

HARMONIZE: TO INTEGRATE THE EIGHT STEPS INTO DAY-TO-DAY COMMUNITY RELATIONSHIPS IN A WAY THAT PREVENTS NEW CONFLICTS AND HEALS OLD ONES.

He described to me how he worked with child soldiers.

The world over, there are military groups who have seen fit to use children to kill in war. Millions of children have been turned into successful killers because they are easily led and manipulated and have little regard for their own personal safety. Also, weapons manufacturers have made extremely deadly guns lighter and lighter, so children can handle them. The terrorist armies kill the parents, or sometimes they make the children kill the parents, and then they own them. Some children have been seen mowing down groups with one arm while cradling a teddy bear in the other. These child soldiers have become the scourge of Africa, an outcast group who no one wants after the war is over. Sam, as a minister, is interested in outcasts.

Sam told me about how warlords, the very people who put guns and teddy bears in their hands, become like fathers to some of these children. This affects Sam deeply. As a person of immense empathy, he feels everything profoundly, which is central to why he is such a brilliant healer. Even as he is revolted by what these kids have done in war, and struggles against their behavior, he at the same time feels boundless empathy for them. They know it, they feel it, and they especially appreciate it because often their own communities and families do not want them back, having suffered so badly from their genocidal behavior.

After working with Sam for a while, some ex-soldiers told him that now Sam is their father. Even though they have been tempted to go back to the military by terrorists and warlords, they will not because of him.

Sam has his own children, but when he heard the word *father* from these unwanted orphan-killers, it moved him. I marvel at Sam's capacity to care for these kids and how he did it in the context of his tragic past, which he reluctantly revealed to me when we were working on solutions for the conflicts of the people of his country. Several years ago I used to run a small nonprofit company that distributed funds to people just like Sam, forward-thinking peacemakers trying to make a difference. Together we were conceiving of a project that could integrate some themes of African healing and reconciliation into the actual restoration of some African villages. I can still see him sitting across from me in my living room in Washington, D.C. Sam is a beautiful African, with profound, wistful eyes, a perpetually easygoing countenance that has earned him the nickname "Smiling Sam," and a soft voice that gets even softer when he must tell a tale of suffering.

Sam described in detail several tribes before the war and how each had its own territory in a remote region of Liberia. He carefully mapped out on paper exactly where each tribe was and then described one small tribe in particular. He explained that it was surrounded by other tribes on all sides and that it ended up being decimated by the war, caught in between strikes and counterstrikes. The small tribe tried to stay out of the war between the other tribes but it was impossible.

He said that many of them had fled into the bush but that no one has heard from them since. Only ten thousand could be found now, and I asked how many had there been before the war, and he said that there had been ninety thousand. That meant that 90 percent of this tribe was missing and there was a good chance they were dead; in other words, this was genocide. He pointed on the map to the name of this tribe, and without looking at me he said quietly, "That is my tribe." I looked him in the eye on that day in my apartment at my dining room table, overlooking the beautiful trees of Rock Creek Park, and then I asked him to repeat what he had said. This time he looked me in the eye: "That is my tribe."

I wanted to scream at that moment. I had never seen Sam, before that moment, as a victim and survivor of enormous violence. I had always seen him and often counted on him as a powerful peacemaker. Here was this man working tirelessly with killers, engaging their needs and inner lives, but he was also vulnerable, robbed of his community and culture. So much of what he knew as a child was gone.

Sam is one of the resilient people walking on this earth, those rare human beings who can survive the worst catastrophes and even flourish. Such human beings teach the rest of us how to evolve our personalities despite tragedy. It is clear that this involves much more than the acquisition of skills of healing; it involves self-healing, a harmony of traits that presents a powerful model to others confronting the same difficult circumstances.

I have read reports from Sam's organization, including a story of how another peacemaker in that group, who we will call Emanuel, described a seminar with ex-child soldiers and how difficult it is to work with these ex-soldiers, ex-children, whom no one wants. Emanuel remembers how unruly the children were during the two-day seminar and how nothing seemed to work to get them to focus. He finally decided to just "speak to their hearts." So he did, for two days. He told them about his own life and struggles, and they listened as if in a trance. Children love stories—in fact we all do, but children admit to it—and it seems likely that these children had never seen before an adult model of a good person, or the inner workings of a benevolent heart. They needed to truly see and experience the inner life of an adult who could teach them how to feel the pain of another while at the same time feeling their own pain.

Nothing replaces the importance of character as we confront extreme injury. Character entails the ability to integrate and harmonize all the steps that we have outlined and then relate with compassion to others who stand before us. For these kids, first and foremost, it meant seeking and finding new parents so that they could once again be children in search of structure, but this time a moral, loving structure. They regained, if only somewhat, their childhood, their innocence, their parents. These new parents moved them to live in the world in a less violent way. It did not solve all their problems, but it gave them a new way to be that was the beginning of a long journey.

For people like Sam and Emanuel, their character allows them to live in violent situations while maintaining their capacity for love. They share themselves with these kids, reaching deep down into their personalities to find the strength to work with killers.

Developing the kind of character that it takes to make peace and harmonize with others is the final step in healing. It integrates and perfects all the other steps toward healing that we have taken. You can have all the training in the world in managing and solving conflicts, but if you have not come to know your own inner life, and if you have not worked on your own character, then all the skills in the world will not help you heal the conflicts around you.

Speaking to the Heart

Sam's core character traits are the key to his success as a peacemaker and a survivor of conflicts. He has a deep well of love, even for those whose actions he despises; he accepts himself as a parent to others in need; he is humble; and he is able to truly see and hear the person with whom he sits. Sam also is spontaneous and flexible enough to adjust his ways of interaction to the needs of those before him. He creatively used the lessons of the Eight Steps to heal himself, and now he uses them to heal whole communities.

Emanuel's character is more complicated. When he decided, perhaps somewhat out of frustration, to speak directly to the hearts of those child soldiers for such a long period of time, he violated the unspoken norms of the field of conflict resolution. Generally the practices of conflict resolution and mediation focus on how we can intervene in other people's conflict by facilitating their dialogues or by training that allows them to see their conflicts in a new frame on their own. But instead of role-playing, simulations, or other "empowering" methods of training, Emanuel spoke from his heart, not just for few minutes, but over a period of days. He saw that these poor, lost kids needed his story, the inner workings of his heart, and so he gave it to them, and it worked, it calmed them down. He told them a story with which they could empathize and that could help them escape, however briefly, their inner turmoil. He managed to capture their attention and their hearts by creating a space for them to listen about how to coexist with others. Emanuel also saw that these kids needed a model of nonviolent normalcy, someone who experienced pain and loss but did not kill as a result. Emanuel's approach required spontaneity, but it also required something much deeper. He had to reach into his inner life in a way that would move those children to change deeply.

No one but the most rigid would fault Emanuel for taking this chance with the kids, but it required great courage on his part nevertheless. Emanuel had to expose his deepest self and his own story to a group of hardened ex-soldiers who could have really hurt him in return. Emanuel made his own character into an ally of the hardest work in healing that Africa faces today, and for that courage his work would be admired by everyone who knew of it.

Likewise, our own character is central as a means of healing ourselves and reaching the inner life of people who are in pain around us. This is especially true in any relationship in which we are called upon to be role models for others, such as between parents and children or teachers and students. We tend to assume that the best way to learn is for youngsters to listen to what the teacher and other adults say and how they say it. In fact, most learning comes from an observation of these authority figures as role models, what we have called See. See and Hear, exercised by these kids as they watched Emanuel, is what led to their transformation. Sam and Emanuel are doing remarkable work that is showing excellent results with most of the children.

Many of us act the rebel when we are put in a passive situation of learning. We don't really want to be consciously molded by anyone, and so we resist many things we learn in class. At the same time, young people are insecure about how they should live and who they should be, and so they quietly look for models. They are always looking and curious, even if they conceal this and will never admit it to you.

I noticed this in remarkable ways when I was in parochial school as a boy. The teachers who lectured endlessly, harangued students, and constantly scolded are only remembered now for their capacity for intimidation. One of my teachers, Rabbi Citron, was different. He was by no means a pushover; he let you know when he thought you were doing the wrong thing. What makes him beloved by so many students to this day, though, is the artful way in which he could tell you off and show you how much he loved you at the same time. It was the love that we remember, and the accompanying guilt at failing to do what he wanted you to do, even thirty years later!

Rabbi Citron had a habit of going up to you and faking corporeal punishment. He would grab you around the shoulders ever so gently, like a hug, and say, in his inimitable German accent, "And where is your homework, Mr. Gopin?" Then he would fake a growl that would send us into hysterics. I can still hear it. He would translate our names from their English or German etymology into Hebrew words that were funny, calling on you in class with the funny name. You had to laugh and pay attention all at once. Some teachers yelled to get our attention, whereas he would whisper, and, miraculously, it always worked. There was a mysterious strength to this unusual Holocaust survivor. You just wanted to be good in his presence.

What I also remember from several of my best teachers in those years is not what they taught me, but how they thought through intellectual and moral problems in front of us. This was true of Rabbi Citron. Their minds and their hearts were on display—that was the mechanism behind their teaching, and it mattered more than the substance of their instruction. We learned from who they were, not what they taught. It was a life lesson that went well beyond a formal education to encompass all human encounters.

When we consider this technique from the perspective of conflict resolution, it means that who we are sometimes has a far greater impact on our adversaries than what we say or do, no matter how persuasive we try to be with our words or gestures. I can vouch for this; sometimes who I am as a person can impact a desperate situation when no amount of professional process or skill can help. I have witnessed violent conflicts where compromise between sides was impossible and where rational conversations barely existed. In such situations, personal friendships, loyalties, and love can cut across impossibly high boundaries. In such situations, some extraordinary people have managed to integrate every skill and moral quality that we have analyzed in the Eight Steps and harmonize them into some basic life decisions about friendship and commitment. This integration can carry relationships through rough waters until opportunities for healing arise. This is the essence of Harmonize.

Reaching Out to Adversaries

I can think of one particular moment that changed my inner life. I passed a message from one enemy, an Israeli, to another, a Palestinian, over the telephone. Both were soldiers whom I had known for a number of years. They became close friends as they worked behind the scenes for peace with each of their political leaders. I then became close with both of them as we worked together on the political leaders. These two men lived three thousand miles away from me, but one of them was visiting me in Boston in order to continue working in the United States on educating people about the situation. Here were two people who lived just ten miles from each other on the West Bank of Israel, who loved each other as friends, who were powerless to stop the violence, and who were wedded indelibly to political, military, and ideological structures that pitted them against each other. Many forces were beyond their capacity to change, but *they* were in charge of their relationship.

I remember being in my family home, sitting in my children's toy room, and viewing the sunset through colored foliage, distracting me from the difficulty of conveying this message on the phone. For various reasons, it was too dangerous for one of them to speak directly on the phone. I passed on greetings and some veiled, subtle messages about plans to try to push peace forward. I sat listening and transferring the communications. Then came precise words, from one warrior to another, "Tell him that I love him."

Something broke inside me when I heard those words, and something was also born. At that moment, other practical attempts to improve the situation simply lay still inside me, in silent reverence before these words as they caught me off guard. I had expected a strategic message, a message about further meetings, or some political statement, because words of the heart can cut like a knife when you know that war and death swirl around the people you love.

I remember feeling that my role was strange and yet sacred. It was as if I were catching a glimpse of some truth about the human condition that I would have never seen if it were not for such an unusual web of friendships that I had cultivated. It was a privilege—but it was also a horror because it is easier to condemn haters and bigots who cause wars and commit human rights violations. So many people I know distance themselves from the warriors because it is easier to condemn and not face the difficult reality of their humanity. It is harder to accept the tragedy of people who care for each other but are caught up in political and military machines of mutual destruction. Yet there they are. There we are as a human race, all too often. If these two men could be like this with each other, with such affection, after so many had died, and after they themselves had barely escaped harm so often, then anything is possible.

It was just one moment, but just one moment is sometimes all that is needed to set us on a better path with greater meaning in our lives and greater wisdom in our hearts. I learned from these two men the power of heroism in and through friendship, even in the most radical circumstances of war. I learned the importance of opening up your inner life to healing relationships and reaching out to adversaries when everything else has failed. I learned that who I am in the moment of encounter with another human being is more important than any idea I may have about how to solve a problem. That does not mean that I should not cultivate skills of problem solving with my adversaries, but it does mean that if they could salvage love and friendship even in the midst of war, then most certainly I can try to do that in my personal conflicts.

Accepting the Bad with the Good

I have wondered for a long time why it is so hard for us to express love to adversaries. Perhaps it is for the same reason that it is so difficult to feel love for ourselves, because it is hard to accept partial hatred and partial love. It is hard to accept that you love parts of who you are and what you have become and hate other parts at the same time. Self-examination can help with this, but many people must blame others for anything that is wrong with themselves. Conversely, they may get depressed because they feel the opposite: They find it hard *not* to condemn themselves completely when something important in life does not work out.

In the same way it is much easier to condemn someone absolutely while considering others completely innocent. This helps explain why, for example, loving parents can fly into a rage at a child they love and care for constantly. In their anger they simply cannot hold on to a complex picture of their child. The child is suddenly everything that is wrong with their life, an exact incarnation of everything I hate about my father, destroying the family, and other such horrible thoughts. This kind of simplification is typical among strong adversaries.

The subtlety of making bad judgments and good ones at the same time does not come easily to us. We must work hard at it and develop some basic habitual inner messages that occur to us in these crunch moments when we lose patience. These are times of great tension and emotional upset, when it is easy for conflict to become dehumanizing, or when it is so easy to lose our capacity to love others.

The two soldier friends, one Israeli and one Palestinian, taught me how to hold together good and bad judgments. They were both well aware of the flaws inside their ideological camps, and they were well aware of the bad human behavior of many involved. They certainly would disagree about the details of long-term solutions being proposed politically, and yet they were so committed to each other and their families. This commitment meant that they would always be reliable peace partners. Their committed friendship and love was more durable than the technical challenges of finding compromises and solutions. What it required of them personally was an integration of all their capacities as healers. They had taken the step of harmonizing their relations.

One of the key elements of their conversations that I noticed was the intensity of the listening and the openness to each other's worlds. Listening to others for extended periods is a great discipline, and we have covered this in the step Hear. Now we must take this and integrate it with Harmonize.

Entering into the world of others, in general, is enormously helpful to inner growth. Reading great literature, for example, helps put a mirror up to our own inner lives and at the same time enter into the lives of others. In Herman Melville's novel *Moby Dick* we learn from Captain Ahab about why and when people become obsessed to such a degree that they destroy everything around them. We can see aspects of our own character in Captain Ahab. Many of us have a great whale whose pursuit has spurred us on in life, given us a mission, and at the same time beguiled us with disappointment and frustration. The "great whale" starts off as a great goal but ends up as a destructive burden.

In Melville's *Billy Budd* we also can see part of ourselves, a good man thrust into an awful situation who becomes the object of hatred precisely because he is so good. Many of us have that experience from time to time. This kind of hatred happens often in competitive families. We must beware of acquiescing to other people's hatreds. Entering into the world of another through great literature is a valuable way to approach this work.

Direct contact with a wide spectrum of human beings is the greatest and most challenging spur to harmonizing your life with others. The more diverse those we listen to and study, the more we develop patience for and creativity in human conflict. My training in several religious traditions suggests that making yourself anonymous in the process of listening to others is the best way to go, visiting places and cultures where you are not known is helpful—this can be a pub just down the street!

Listening is helpful in forgetting yourself, forgetting your frame of reference for a time, so you may come back to yourself and integrate what you have learned. The same can be done in the context of your conflicts—a cognitive and emotional cease-fire of sorts that opens up avenues of wisdom and personal growth.

Listening at All Costs

Another one of my international students, Father Joseph, provides a powerful model for harmonizing our lives. Joseph is a religious man who barely managed to survive the genocide in Rwanda. Joseph is a Tutsi; many of the people he knew were slaughtered by Hutus, along with eight hundred thousand other Tutsi and moderate Hutus.

At a certain point in the confusion of war, Joseph found himself just over the border of Rwanda, in a refugee camp. He was mistaken for Hutu and he merged anonymously into a bastion of Hutu militia men. This accident was the most terrifying situation that one can imagine for a survivor of genocide, but that is exactly what happened. Amazingly enough, he did not just run for his life but instead developed a curiosity about his enemies as he stayed in the camp.

Joseph remembers nights around campfires where the Hutu men would compare how many Tutsi men, women, and children they had slaughtered, laughing and joking. Joseph held himself back from saying a word. It is not clear to me that he did this to save his life, because from what I could tell he could escape the camp at any time. The truth is that he was fascinated and curious. It was not a morbid curiosity, and it was not even a scientific curiosity about the inner psychological lives and social interaction of mass murderers. No, for Joseph it was a spiritual path. Joseph needed to understand the full face of the human condition, and he truly needed to understand the heart of his enemy. He was trying to make sense of the hell that he had endured.

Joseph needed to understand these men who killed innocents and yet who had normal human interactions and family lives. Joseph did not just hear horror stories, he also heared the good side of some of these people. It was torturous and enlightening all at once, and he came to see the good and evil that reside together in the human breast, the utter failure of humanity and its capacity for goodness all at the same time.

This path gave Joseph a way out of hell, a way to see the enemy as flawed, human, and capable of change under better circumstances. These are lessons that in his wounded state he did not necessarily want to learn. It would have been much easier to condemn the killers all to hell, every one of them. The silence and the listening required of Joseph a more nuanced response to this most extreme situation. It changed him as a person; it made him develop his capacity for dealing with conflict into a way of truly living, more than he had ever experienced before.

As a pious Christian, Joseph had preached love for his fellow human beings, following the model of Jesus, who extended his love even to his enemies. For Joseph, a case of mistaken identity and an experiment in dangerous anonymity led him face to face with this most difficult practice. It led him down a path of silence, humility, and healing.

If Joseph could do this in the midst of genocide, then why should we not follow this discipline when we are injured in less violent ways by parents, by our children, by partners, and by colleagues? Joseph has many grievances about

Rwanda, and he is particularly angry that the Catholic Church did not do its utmost to stamp out the racism that infected its hierarchy prior to the genocide. And yet he learned about the heart and soul of his enemy, and it taught him things about the human condition and even about himself.

The lesson here is to find ways to know and listen to those whom you're in conflict with; this can be constructive for you. Even military strategists, from Sun Tsu to Clausewitz, see the logic in this approach. The more of everyone's story, of the human story, that we hold inside our hearts and minds, the stronger we become. This harmonizing path fulfills us personally in a way that will survive the successes and failures of our attempts to heal conflicts in our lives and in our communities.

Making Space for Others

Being comfortable with the space that we occupy at the same time that we allow for the comfort and happiness of others is one of the great tasks of being in harmony. Our lives from the beginning are almost programmed for conflict over space. We are born into situations of complete dependency; in the best of circumstances infants get used to a great deal of attention and the centralization of all available resources on themselves. At this point in our lives we take up all the "space" of the family's resources. Fairly soon, however, we have to share space with others, and the competition for attention becomes fierce. Parents come under pressure from siblings to give back the space and time that they took for the newborn.

The best evidence of how much space a newborn takes up is how quickly older siblings regress into acting like babies themselves. They long for the kind of attention and unconditional love that the baby receives. I used to think that sibling rivalry was a minor annoyance, but now that I have young children I see it as the essential struggle of human beings to make space for themselves and to recover from injury at space that has been lost. Not a few parents have talked to me about how their second child spends day and night competing with the first one. Very young children in this circumstance say and do radical things, including wishing siblings dead or wishing to disown their families. Then they have to deal with the guilt they feel over those violent thoughts and statements.

Later in life we often see adults behaving the same way once someone new has joined a committee, for example, or a workplace, and is able to fill the same role or do the same task that they can. The tension can be immense because someone else is threatening the legitimacy of your existence.

It is critical to recognize space and time as scarce, precious resources that we are called upon to share. It is also critical to teach and model for a family or a community the capacity to negotiate these scarce resources with an artful combination of fairness, justice, love, and compassionate tolerance for the inevitable imperfections of these efforts. The road is inherently bumpy, but it is the foundation of taking the lessons of the Eight Steps into the construction of community.

There are two opposite tasks when it comes to sharing space: one is making others feel welcome to the space, and the other is making those who already are in the space feel that they have not been dislodged.

Humankind has been facing these challenges for thousands of years, and so it makes sense to draw on ancient wisdom to understand what works best. There are two complementary principles that are critical here to the balance involved in sharing space: tradition and the rule of law and the welcoming of guests and strangers. The ritual honoring of guests is an ancient sacred practice in every major culture and religion in the world. By contrast, tradition and the rule of law, also expressed throughout the world in culture and religion, teach that the standards by which a community lives guarantee the rights of those who already occupy a certain space. In other words, no matter how welcoming you may be of strangers, you cannot forget the rights of those who already constitute the community. Laws of property rights and ownership must be upheld so that people will not feel overrun by foreigners.

One little-known book of the Hebrew Bible illustrates this delicate balance. *The Book of Ruth* tells the compelling story of a Jewish woman named Naomi who must leave the Holy Land with her husband and two sons due to a famine. They travel to the land of Moab, traditionally an enemy of the people of Israel. The famine is widespread, however, and Naomi's husband and her two sons die of starvation. She is left with two Moabite daughters-in-law and no children. Naomi persuades one to go back to her people, but Ruth persists and loves Naomi so much that she declares that she will never leave her and will instead link herself to Naomi's destiny.

Ruth becomes a model of devotion, sacrifice, and spiritual friendship. When they both return to the Holy Land as two vulnerable and childless women, a remarkable person, Boaz, steps forward. Boaz makes sure that his workers treat Ruth the Moabite woman with respect and kindness. Ruth is the ultimate stranger in a strange land, but Boaz demonstrates the spiritual significance of loving the stranger, of taking her in and treating her as an equal. Eventually Boaz will marry Ruth and carry on the name of Naomi's dead husband in a remarkable gesture of generosity. But here is the point: Before Boaz does this he strictly adheres to the laws of the time and makes sure that no other heirs have any claims.

The Book of Ruth demonstrates a commitment to two values simultaneously: the love and embrace of strangers to share space and the commitment to rules and order in order to honor those who already live in social contract with each other.

We can learn a great deal from this story about negotiating space with adversaries. Making everyone feel absolutely welcome, especially through time-honored rituals, is a critical way to "enlarge" the space we live in. At the same time, we must not dishonor or dislodge those who have come before.

In families, it is critical for there to be rituals of inclusion for new members, but they must be accompanied at all times by ways in which those who are already there feel honored, welcomed, loved, and guaranteed the place that they had before. This does not mean that older siblings do not have to go through mourning over lost space. They will and it is natural. But our job is to skillfully shape the family community, and the community at large, to harmonize everything that we have learned about healing conflict.

The Book of Ruth ends on a happy note, with Naomi being admired by everyone in town because of Ruth's love for her. Naomi and Ruth become the ancestors of King David. They represent in the Bible the triumph of devotion and love, while Boaz represents the power and importance of welcoming the stranger, making space for others, while honoring traditions and customs at the same time. It adds up to a beautiful story of communal harmony and restoration, despite the backdrop of famine and the loss of children.

Between Patience and Passion

I have rarely met a person who successfully helps people resolve conflicts who does not have a great deal of passion. We tend to think of peace as a static phenomenon, a state of rest, but it is hardly that. It is a dynamic process of interaction that requires constant activity, creativity, and a relentless desire for connection. It requires a kind of energy that is optimistic at its core but committed to looking at the heart of conflict. There is a dogged determination to face the problems that everyone else avoids combined with a great deal of patience. The passion does not spill over into impatience and intolerance but rather translates into a determination to make one's efforts into a way of life, a way of being in the world.

Senator George Mitchell is one of the great peacemakers of our time. What has struck me most in my brief encounters with him has been the sparkle in his eye when he speaks of a path to peace for Ireland or the Middle East, as if it is his deepest longing. At the same time his delivery of ideas and recommendations are sober, patient, and measured in every word.

What Senator Mitchell can teach us on a personal level is to condition ourselves to face problems with a kind of passionate optimism, as if they are an opportunity. We rarely have those feelings late at night, exhausted and discouraged by a bad day. At times like that we should attach ourselves to loved ones and favorite things. In the morning, when our energy is up and we can look at things in a fresh way, it is vital to access our natural energy and gear it toward a passion for peacemaking, almost a faith that part of our day can be spent on healing at least one part of one important relationship. In this way conflict resolution becomes a vocation and a calling.

In Judaism, peace is not just a goal, it is a sacred passion, something that God wishes for everyone. Peace should be something that we consider a passion, an approach that does not make our conflict any less severe but does strengthen our determination, our sense of hope, and our power of perseverance.

As I said at the beginning of the book, conflict is a basic part of life. Many conflicts are constructive and healthy, yielding benefits of personal transformation. One of the keys to turning potentially destructive conflicts into constructive ones is being committed to the idea of conflict as an opportunity to actually strengthen human relations.

As I have gotten older I have come to expect that some of the things I do and say will make people uncomfortable, such as things that I may say on the radio or television about difficult global conflicts. Anticipating these reactions has made me a far more tolerant person than I was twenty years ago. I react with a little more compassion now because I have much greater sympathy for typical human reactions to conflict and violence. It is my passion that has led me to much more creative responses to others, but it is a work in progress. If I am hurt by someone unexpectedly and am caught off guard, I may not seize the moment constructively.

If you learn to anticipate conflicts and have the passion to address them head-on, then you can imagine in advance what you are going to do about it, which can yield better relations in the long run. Think about what has worked best in the past. Rather than mourn over the loss of what was, embrace the changes conflict brings and find the opportunities to heal yourself and others in the process.

Care and Love

Rarely do I find among the great healers of conflicts someone who has trouble expressing emotions. Most of the great women and men in this line of work are people who care deeply about the people they are trying to help. That is how they make it so easy for people to pass through the step of Feel, because it is a natural way for them to be, full of the positive emotions of care and love.

To find feelings of care and love even in the middle of your worst conflicts is extremely demanding, and that is why I have reserved discussion of it until now. We all know the bickering spouse syndrome, that odd way in which human beings can sometimes turn conflict on and off like a faucet. "You are the most selfish person I have ever come across! You always forget anything that I want at the store." Then, five minutes later, "Honey, do you want some of my popcorn, I made extra?" as if nothing ever happened. A witness to the scene, perhaps a guest in the house, thinks he has stumbled onto the beginning of a divorce and wonders why anyone ever gets married, but it is just another evening at home. Care and love merge together with conflict.

Now this is not the most ideal situation in human relations, but neither is it entirely destructive. It is rather the venting of stress and frustration coupled with absolute care and commitment. On the other hand, we should not trivialize the difficulty of doing this in a way that does not yield destructive results, nor should we blindly apply this approach to destructive conflicts.

For me it has been important to gauge my responses to catastrophic conflict on role models. The Israeli and Palestinian soldiers have become models for me of how to love and care in the midst of war. I look to Sam to help me feel certain things about enemies because he has capabilities that I do not easily have, at least when it comes to empathizing with violent people. Role models have a magnetic effect on all of us, and actively seeking them out is a powerful way to learn how to care for others even in the worst of circumstances.

I had heard about Sheikh Said even before I met him on the West Bank. He was known to be a man who preached love, a religious leader who danced sacred dances with Jews and Muslims alike. I imagined him in my mind before I met him, and I was determined to return his gestures of peace to his enemies.

I do not think I have ever connected so closely with another man in my life, even though we are ostensibly enemies. In the worst of times we have embraced and sung songs together, offered each other words of comfort and inspiration, sometimes from three thousand miles away. In fact, when I made phone calls to him in the midst of war they were some of the most intense encounters that we had. You never know who is desperately seeking care among your adversaries, and sometimes the smallest gestures can create a revolution in relationships. Sheikh Said has sustained my hopes and dreams for peace, and I have helped in a small way to sustain his, but he has had the courage to provide the model for me and thousands of others.

The capacity for love and care does not preclude and is not meant to suppress our sense of justice and fairness. It is a basic lesson of healing conflicts that we cannot and should not ignore basic concerns for justice. The love and care that help us harmonize do not preclude the need to pass judgment occasionally, to reject behaviors as criminal and deserving of prison or punishment.

Judgment has to be weighed in the balance, however, with the overriding goal of inducing a steady decline in the destructiveness of our conflicts and a steady increase in its constructive aspects. Ignoring basic issues of right and wrong while completely favoring love is a violation of a necessary balancing act of our inner moral compass and outer moral codes. Rather, as with so much of our program here, balance is needed between competing characteristics that make up the personality of the person who successfully resolves her own conflicts. There is no choice sometimes but to struggle with this balance, and to err slightly on one side or the other, depending on what the circumstances demand.

Honesty, Dishonesty, Acknowledgment

Such critical choices demand another key trait of our capacity to harmonize: honesty. Honesty, like all aspects of character, is to be considered as a work in progress. None of these steps are effective or useful if we see them as something static, a thing that we either have or lack. All of these qualities are ideals toward which we are always aspiring, like the center of a target. It is by aiming at the center of the target that we make progress toward healing. Every gesture of honesty and acknowledgment has a remarkable effect on the system of interactions that enemies have with each other.

I have a friend and colleague, Tara, who is an excellent communicator with even the most difficult people. She has the remarkable capacity to easily acknowledge anything she may have done that misled others in conversation, and in fact she seems ready at every moment to acknowledge her role in miscommunication. I have noticed this trait in a number of people, including my sister Reissa, who excels at this in her business communications. She has a remarkable strength of character that allows her to take responsibility in a way that completely disarms the people with whom she is communicating.

In any conflict it is highly likely that there will be many misunderstandings for which both parties are responsible, principally because communication is a highly imprecise process. Undoubtedly some people are worse at straightforward communication than others, and many are downright deceptive. By simply acknowledging the basic truth of common miscommunications, however, Tara and Reissa create more harmonious relationships. Some people go through their entire lives never apologizing for anything. That is a mark of great weakness and dishonesty.

There are two aspects to honesty: one is honesty with ourselves, and the other is honesty with others, and both are critical habits to develop. There is a problem with honesty, however, that directly affects conflict and how we heal our relationships. The truth is that I am often "dishonest" with adversaries about certain things, in the sense that I do not necessarily communicate everything I know. When I intervene, for example, in someone else's conflict, I don't provoke people by telling them the worst of what their opponents have said to me about them. When I am in a fight with someone I am always trying to hold back as well, trying to resist making matters worse by saying everything that is in my heart. Resisting complete candor is not necessarily destructive; on the contrary, it seems often to be necessary.

Distinguishing between when honesty is productive in solving conflicts and when it is destructive is a difficult and imperfect art. The whole method in conflict resolution of reframing, which means helping two people or groups work out their problems by restating their positions in more constructive ways, is a bit deceptive as a practice. After all, many people say things in destructive ways precisely because they are feeling and intending to be destructive! So why reframe it? They may, in the moment of encounter, *want* to hurt or humiliate. When we reframe what they are saying in more positive terms, are we not being somewhat dishonest? I think so. Nevertheless, reframing has its virtues, as long as it does not deliberately cover up anger that needs to be expressed.

We should censor ourselves to some degree but not to the point of suppressing the heart of the conflict. People have to get to know much ugliness before they can look past it to an authentic transformation of relationship. Honesty is good and important in many ways but destructive when it is gratuitous, cruel, and, especially, endless. There is a time and a place for hurtful honesty, and then there is a time to end it and move on to constructive relationship building. This balance is one of the keys to achieving the goals of Harmonize.

How to decide what is appropriate in terms of candor often depends on the skill and moral character of everyone involved. It is in the inner workings of good character that we balance competing values, all of which are good and right. It is inside the good personality that truth is balanced with compassion or with honor, for example, or humility with confident empowerment, or the pursuit of peace with the pursuit of justice. Good character is critical to our capacity to know how and when to maximize the benefits of truth to resolving our conflicts. Harmonize asks us to work on practicing that balance on a regular basis, experimenting with it, and learning from our failures.

Empathy

Empathy has a special relationship to the goal of harmonizing. It is in some ways the essence of peacemaking and the healing of conflicts, for it is in the experience of empathy that we discover new ways to coexist with others in a community. It is both a liberating and baffling moment, ridden with a feeling of crisis for many people. To understand both our own needs and those of someone who is actively opposing us or hating us is an agonizing moment of truth, a moment in which the world seems to be a flawed and tragic place of contradiction. Yet the cultivation and experience of empathy is also a place of truth, as well as one of the most powerful goads to creativity known to human beings.

It has been said that necessity is the mother of invention. In conflict, once you really know your own heart, and when you come to know the heart of someone or some group that hates you, you feel compelled to invent or discover a third way of existence, a way of coexistence. A decent world, a good world, can bear no other solution. Thus empathy paves the way for powerful skills of creativity to develop inside of us.

Thich Nhat Hanh is one of the great peace theologians of our time. Hanh writes frequently about the Buddhist principle of non-dualism. It is his way of expressing the basic idea that a true consciousness of reality eliminates the separation between you and me. We are the same, and he trains himself and others in a discipline of getting our minds used to this reality.

Hanh's idea is essentially the same as empathy. What is so important about Hanh's approach is that he has shown, through the training of thousands of students, that empathy, or non-dualism, is a habit of the heart that can be cultivated. Tens of thousands of Vietnamese citizens, escaping from that troubled country by boat, were set upon by pirates, and unspeakable atrocities occurred. The world refused to take in these people, and Thich Nhat Hanh and many others generated global protests on their behalf, demanding that countries such as the United States open its borders to these refugees. Eventually the United States and others did, but not before many Vietnamese were killed or drowned.

Hanh wrote an astonishing poem in which he identifies with a raped little girl among the boat people. He says at one point in the poem, "I am the raped girl . . . ," and he proceeds to tell the tale of how someone becomes a Vietnamese girl who is raped and loses her life on the high seas. Then, in a shocking move, he goes on with the poem and writes, "I am the pirate . . . ," and he proceeds to tell the tale of how someone becomes a desperate, angry pirate on the high seas. It is an empathetic tale of the tragic meeting of destinies, and we the readers are left speechless by it, moved to understand the power and necessity of empathy in order to truly challenge and undermine the roots of human tragedy and violence.

Hanh does not stop at pious phrases of love for humankind but instead enters into the dark essence of human tragedy and insists on taking empathy into that dark place. He insists on illuminating for us the joys and the sorrows of a young girl's short life, as well as the self-hating misery of a pirate. He insists on doing this not in order to generate outrage, as too much Western social criticism does, but in order to generate the empathy and identification with others that will lead us to save little girls from rape and save little boys from growing up to be rapists.

Suzy is a fabulous healer. On a professional level she engages in massage therapy that is designed to help victims of chronic diseases affecting the use of their limbs. She sees many people in pain and demonstrates a great capacity to empathize with them. Suzy had become more and more troubled by the persistent wars in the world that are rooted in ethnic hatred, and so she got involved with an important African AIDS activist, Omekongo, who works with orphaned children. This man has suffered many personal tragedies, as most of his original village and family were wiped out by AIDS, he being one of the few survivors. He is a driven, brilliant man in his fifties who knows how to work political and economic systems to press for change and save lives. Yet he is driven by impatience and guilt at the endless loss of life.

As I heard how difficult Omekongo can be to work with, I became interested in how Suzy was successfully negotiating this relationship. The relationship was critical to the continuation of this vital work, and yet I wondered whether it was sustainable.

One day Suzy and I were discussing her dealings with Omekongo. We were talking about making plans for him, and she mentioned in passing, "Of course, he won't do that. He can't be in such a meeting without saying those angry things. He needs to say those things because of his mourning." Then she immediately went on to another topic.

What struck me about that conversation was how much Suzy had internalized empathy as a habit of her thinking and dealing with Omekongo, as if it had become second nature. Everyone else ended up fighting with this man, but Suzy was so brilliant and quick at empathy that you could easily miss why she was helping a complicated but good man in ways that no one else could. She had radical empathy, but not in some spiritual moment of emotional inspiration. Rather this was a habit of her heart that led to her uniquely effective style of strategizing and negotiating. Suzy had a sustainable relationship with Omekongo because of her empathy, but there was only so much she could do for him, as it was he who had to ultimately face many questions about himself in order to not continually ruin his relationships.

Defying the Past to Compose the Good Life

As we have seen earlier, it is easy to become addicted to conflict as a way of life, but this need not be so. We can compose a different life, one that does not solve all the problems of the past but that does directly transform the worst of the past into the ingredients for a better future.

Pedro provides an excellent example. Pedro is a highly educated man from a small village in Central America. He now lives in the United States, but still he is saddened every day by news of the injustices being suffered by the people in his village. He knows exactly who is perpetrating these injustices, and he feels as powerless as the villagers to change the situation. It plagues him doubly because the whole reason that he got educated in the first place was to figure out how to improve the lives of people just like those back home.

Pedro became a lawyer, a very good one. He helps people all the time with difficult problems that they cannot solve, but he cannot help the people in his old village. When he helps people here, Pedro knows that the best negotiators get everyone to do the right thing, thinking all the while that they have gained the most from the creative compromises developed. He protects the defenseless so artfully that even the most oppressive litigants think they have won at the end of the process. It does not always go this smoothly, but it does so often enough to give him a fabulous reputation.

When Pedro returns for visits to his family in the village, all the old rage comes back to him and he loses all his skills. When he meets those in town who oppress his people he feels nothing but contempt, and he has trouble hiding it. Over the years he has become more and more clever at covering his rage, but it is betrayed in his complete inability to intervene in any creative way when it comes to his own family's tragedy.

I would argue that Pedro's story is not one of failure with conflict but one of immense success. Imagine that Pedro stays in the village and sees that nothing is helping the situation. He becomes cynical, losing faith in everything. He loses interest in education. To make a little money on the side, he gets involved in petty crime, and this involvement goes on for five years. He is a smart man, so he ends up with his own successful crime gang.

One day he sees an opportunity to marry his petty crime to his abiding rage. He has been looking for more meaning in his life while growing older, some way to leave a lasting mark beyond his reputation as a petty criminal. He never married and has no children and so has no family legacy to leave, but maybe he can leave a name for himself in other ways.

Pedro and his small crime group sabotage a power plant owned by the richest person in town, which will make Pedro's own crime group the only supplier of reliable energy in the form of kerosene oil. This crime will make him wealthy and a hero in one fell swoop. Only, by accident, he kills several workers in the process of blowing up the plant. The incident gets the attention of the national authorities, they hunt him down, he kills some of them, and is eventually killed himself. The army cracks down on the whole village as a result of the cycle of violence, intending to teach a lesson. They exile Pedro's family, and they live as refugees on the border. Pedro is dead and his family is ruined.

Now, Pedro's life as he has truly lived it is a life in which he took a difficult, destructive conflict and turned it into a life mission. He made it a constructive conflict by making *himself* into an agent of positive change for helpless people. Pedro composed a life for himself, a good life of profound meaning. He could not solve the problems of his own village, and he was not terribly good at controlling his anger when he returned there. Yet in most of his life he turned a sad past into an empowered present and future.

Pedro found meaning in conflict, but he turned it into a constructive sort of struggle for the good of defenseless people, which also created a successful professional life. Even more impressively, he is teaching people across the country how to stand up for what is right while simultaneously including all sides in solutions to conflicts. He discovered meaning through struggle, but he made it a struggle that is ultimately healing for everyone. He brings happiness to many people, including to himself.

Pedro does have to face the fact that he is not God, that he loses his skills when in his old village, and that he tends to fight destructively there, not constructively. But, on balance, he is on a good life path and has negotiated a legacy of bitter conflict with great personal skill and moral character.

What we learn from Pedro is how to transform a legacy of destructive conflict into a lifelong legacy of constructive conflict. In some ways we may never let go of the old conflicts, but still we can turn them into something noble, meaningful, and ultimately healing for everyone.

Pedro is in harmony with life. Other people we have introduced in this chapter, such as Sam, Rabbi Citron, the Israeli soldier and the Palestinian soldier, Sheikh Said, Thich Nhat Hanh, and Suzy each has demonstrated the way in which the ultimate goal of healing conflicts is the achievement of a certain way of life that harmonizes all the steps of healing conflicts and forges them into the building blocks of good character. They have created noble and meaningful lives in healing destructive conflict in relationships.

It is a noble thing to walk upon this earth knowing that every day you have tried to train yourself to build relationships rather than destroy them. It is a powerful model that is likely to ease your relationships with many adversaries. Like these conflict healers, by following the Eight Steps you may discover a greater state of peace as you face the continuing challenges of the human condition.

RESOURCES

A Sampling of Organizations Engaged in Healing Conflicts

Center for World Religions,
Diplomacy and Conflict Resolution
Director, Dr. Marc Gopin
   Engages in practice, research, and education concerning the contribution of world religions to conflict and to peace
George Mason University
3401 North Fairfax Drive
Arlington, VA 22201
Phone (703) 993-4473
Fax (703) 993-1302
www.gmu.edu/departments/crdc

The Compassionate Listening Project
P.O. Box 17
Indianola, WA 98342
Phone (360) 297-2280
Fax (360) 297-6563
www.compassionatelistening.org

Facing History and Ourselves
16 Hurd Road
Brookline, MA 02445
Phone (617) 232-1595
Fax (617) 232-0281
www.facinghistory.org

Hope in the Cities
1103 Sunset Avenue
Richmond, VA 23221
Phone (804) 358-1764
Fax (804) 358-1769
www.hopeinthecities.org

Initiatives of Change
1156 15th Street, NW, Suite 910
Washington, D.C. 20005
Phone (202) 872 9077
Fax (202) 872 9137
www.iofc.org; www.us.initiativesofchange.org

International Center for Religion and Diplomacy
1156 15th St., NW, Suite 910
Washington, D.C. 20005
Phone (202) 331-9404
Fax (202) 872-9137
www.icrd.org

Institute for Multi-Track Diplomacy
1925 North Lynn Street, 12th Floor
Arlington, VA 22209
Phone (703) 528-3863
Fax (703) 528-5776
www.imtd.org

West Africa Peacebuilding Institute
P.O. Box CT 4434
Cantonments, Accra-Ghana
Phone +233-21-221318/221388
Fax +233-21-221735
www.wanep.org/wapi

Academic Institutions Engaged in Research and Practice Related to Healing Conflicts

Institute for Conflict Analysis and Resolution

Advances the understanding of deeply rooted conflicts between individuals, groups, organizations, and communities in the United States and all over the world through research, teaching, practice, and outreach

George Mason University
Mail Stop 4D3
3330 North Washington Boulevard
Arlington, VA 22201
Phone (703) 993-1300
Fax (703) 993-1302
http://icar.gmu.edu

Conflict Transformation Program at Eastern Mennonite University
1200 Park Road
Harrisonburg, VA 22802-2462
Phone (540) 432-4490
Fax (540) 432-4449
www.emu.edu/ctp

The Joan B. Kroc Institute for Peace Studies
at the University of Notre Dame
100 Hesburgh Center for International Studies
P.O. Box 639
Notre Dame, IN 46556
Phone (574) 631-6970
www.nd.edu/~krocinst

ABOUT THE AUTHOR

Marc Gopin is the James H. Laue Professor of Religion, Diplomacy and Conflict Resolution at George Mason University's Institute for Conflict Analysis and Resolution, and the Director of the Institute's Center for Religion, Diplomacy and Conflict Resolution. He has engaged in back-channel diplomacy with political, religious, and military figures on both sides of conflicts, especially in the Middle East. He has lectured on conflict resolution at Harvard, Yale, Columbia, Princeton, and other academic institutions, and he has trained thousands of students in Switzerland, Ireland, India, Israel, and elsewhere around the world in peacemaking strategies for complex conflicts in which religion and culture play a role.

Gopin received his Ph.D. in religious ethics in 1993 from Brandeis University, and received rabbinic ordination from Rabbi Joseph Soloveitchik and Yeshiva University in 1983. He has appeared as a media analyst on CNN, *The Jim Lehrer News Hour*, Israel Radio, National Public Radio, *The Connection*, Voice of America, and the national public radio stations of Sweden, Ireland, and Northern Ireland. He has been published in the *International Herald Tribune*, the *Boston Globe*, and the *Christian Science Monitor* as well as in numerous books and journals, and his work has been featured in articles by the *Times* of London, the Associated Press, Newhouse News Service, United Press International, and others.

Gopin is the author of two previous books, *Between Eden and Armageddon: The Future of World Religions, Violence, and Peacemaking* (Oxford University Press, 2000), and *Holy War, Holy Peace: How Religion Can Bring Peace to the Middle East* (Oxford University Press, 2002). He lives in Virginia.